5 Ingredients

CROCK POT

Cookbook for Beginners

2000+ Days of Everyday Slow Cooker Recipes for Stress-Free, Healthy Meals Made With Just 5 Ingredients or Less!

Anna E. Floyd

CONTENTS

INTRODUCTION	4
Breakfast Recipes	11
Lunch & Dinner Recipes	20
Beef, Pork & Lamb Recipes	29
Poultry Recipes	38
Fish & Seafood Recipes	47
Vegetable & Vegetarian Recipes	56
Snack Recipes	65
Dessert Recipes	74
Conclusion	83
Measurement Conversions	84
HEALTE RECORD TRACKER	86
How to Reduce Food Waste	88
Appendix : Recipes Index	93

INTRODUCTION

The Crock Pot, commonly known as a slow cooker, is a revolutionary kitchen appliance that has transformed the way we prepare and enjoy meals at home. Since its introduction in the 1970s, the Crock Pot has gained immense popularity for its ability to simplify cooking processes and enhance the flavors of a wide variety of dishes. This appliance operates on a straightforward principle: it cooks food at low temperatures over an extended period, allowing ingredients to meld together beautifully and develop rich, deep flavors that are often unattainable with quick cooking methods.

What truly distinguishes the Crock Pot is its remarkable ability to tenderize even the toughest cuts of meat. The low and slow cooking technique breaks down collagen in the meat, resulting in a juicy, flavorful final product that melts in your mouth. This is particularly beneficial for busy families and individuals who appreciate the convenience of setting a meal to cook while they go about their day. With a Crock Pot, you can prepare everything from comforting soups and stews to decadent desserts with minimal hands-on effort, freeing up your time for other activities.

In addition to its practical benefits, the Crock Pot encourages healthier eating habits. Many recipes highlight wholesome ingredients, including fresh vegetables, lean proteins, and whole grains, which contribute to a balanced diet. The extended cooking time allows for better nutrient retention compared to higher-heat methods, making it an excellent choice for those looking to maintain a healthy lifestyle. Today's models come equipped with advanced features such as programmable timers, multiple cooking settings, and even Bluetooth connectivity, making it easier than ever to integrate slow cooking into your routine. Overall, the Crock Pot is more than just a cooking appliance; it represents a lifestyle choice that embraces the joys of home cooking, convenience, and healthy eating.

BENEFITS OF THE CROCK POT

Convenience: One of the primary advantages of using a Crock Pot is the unparalleled convenience it offers to home cooks. Users can simply add their ingredients into the pot in the morning, set the temperature to either low or high, and return home to a hot, ready meal without having to monitor the cooking process continuously. This functionality makes it ideal for busy individuals or families who may not have time to prepare dinner after a long day at work or school. The ability to prepare meals in advance and allow the Crock Pot to do the cooking means that families can enjoy wholesome, nutritious dinners without the stress of last-minute meal preparation or worrying about what to cook after a tiring day.

Moreover, the slow cooking method allows for flexibility in meal planning. You can easily prepare meals in advance and let them cook while you go about your day, whether you're at work, running errands, or taking care of family responsibilities. This not only saves time but also reduces the daily stress of meal planning, enabling families to sit down together and enjoy a warm meal at the end of the day, fostering connection and togetherness.

Flavor Enhancement: One of the standout features of slow cooking is its ability to enhance the flavors of ingredients in a way that is often difficult to achieve through faster cooking methods. Slow cooking allows for the deep infusion of flavors, enabling ingredients like herbs, spices, and aromatics to meld beautifully over several hours, resulting in a rich and flavorful dish that delights the palate. This method is particularly beneficial for tough cuts of meat, which become incredibly tender and succulent when cooked slowly over low heat. The Crock Pot's gentle cooking method allows flavors to develop and intensify, providing a depth and complexity that can elevate a simple recipe into a memorable meal.

Additionally, the low cooking temperatures minimize the risk of burning or overcooking, allowing you to create dishes that are perfectly cooked and full of flavor. Many cooks find that their favorite recipes taste even better when adapted for the Crock Pot, as the long cooking times promote a harmonious blending of flavors that makes every bite a pleasure. The slow cooker is an excellent tool for making hearty stews, savory sauces, and even desserts, showcasing the versatility of this cooking method.

Nutritional Retention:
Another significant benefit of using a Crock Pot is its ability to retain nutritional value in foods. Because slow cooking operates at lower temperatures, it can help preserve more nutrients compared to some traditional cooking methods, such as boiling or frying, which can cause nutrient loss. This can lead to healthier meals, especially when utilizing fresh vegetables, lean proteins, and whole grains. The gentle heat of the Crock Pot prevents the degradation of essential vitamins and minerals that can occur in high-heat cooking methods, making it an excellent option for health-conscious individuals who want to maximize the nutritional value of their meals.

Furthermore, the cooking process often requires less added fat or oil, which contributes to a healthier final dish. When preparing meals in a Crock Pot, you can incorporate a wide variety of wholesome ingredients without the need for excessive seasoning or unhealthy fats. This makes it easier to create nutritious meals that align with dietary preferences and health goals, such as weight loss, heart health, and overall wellness.

Energy Efficiency:
In today's energy-conscious world, the Crock Pot stands out as a remarkably energy-efficient cooking appliance. It typically uses less electricity than an oven, making it a cost-effective choice for meal preparation. This energy efficiency can be particularly beneficial during warmer months when you want to avoid heating up the kitchen with an oven, thus keeping your home cool and comfortable. Cooking in a Crock Pot allows you to prepare satisfying meals without significantly increasing your energy bill, allowing you to enjoy the benefits of home-cooked meals while being mindful of your energy consumption.

Additionally, the low-energy operation of the Crock Pot means you can cook meals for several hours without worrying about excessive electricity use. This makes it an environmentally friendly option for home cooks who are looking to reduce their carbon footprint while still enjoying delicious, home-cooked meals. It is also an ideal choice for slow-cooked meals that simmer gently, creating flavorful dishes without the need for constant attention.

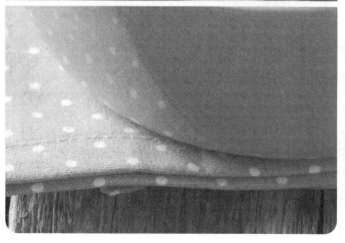

Versatility: The versatility of the Crock Pot is truly one of its most remarkable attributes. It can be used for a wide variety of dishes, including soups, stews, casseroles, and even desserts. This adaptability allows users to experiment with different recipes and cuisines, expanding their culinary repertoire and creativity. From classic comfort foods like chili and beef stew to more adventurous recipes like curries and risottos, the Crock Pot can handle it all, providing a simple solution for feeding a crowd or preparing meals for a busy week ahead.

The wide array of recipes available for slow cooking means that there's something for everyone, whether you're cooking for a family gathering, hosting a dinner party, or simply looking for a cozy meal for yourself. The ability to customize ingredients and adjust cooking times also allows for a great deal of flexibility in preparing dishes that suit various dietary preferences and tastes. For those who enjoy experimenting in the kitchen, the Crock Pot is a valuable tool that encourages creativity and exploration in cooking.

HOW THE CROCK POT WORKS

The Crock Pot is a thoughtfully designed appliance that consists of a ceramic or porcelain pot housed within an outer shell that contains the heating element. Here's a more detailed overview of its operation, which is both simple and effective:

Setup: The cooking process begins with preparing your ingredients. Start by placing your ingredients into the inner pot. It's essential to layer ingredients appropriately, with denser items like potatoes or carrots at the bottom and meats on top to ensure even cooking. This layering helps create a balanced cooking environment, allowing the heat to circulate properly and ensuring that all ingredients cook evenly. When adding liquids, be mindful of the amount; too much liquid can lead to a watery dish, while too little may cause ingredients to stick or burn.

Additionally, consider the order in which you add your ingredients. For example, adding aromatics like onions and garlic at the beginning can help develop their flavors, while delicate ingredients like leafy greens should be added closer to the end of the cooking time to prevent them from becoming overly wilted. Taking the time to prep your ingredients thoughtfully can significantly enhance the final outcome of your dish.

Temperature Settings: Most Crock Pots come equipped with at least two settings: low and high. The low setting typically cooks at around 200°F (93°C), while the high setting operates at about 300°F (149°C). Cooking times can vary depending on the setting chosen and the specific recipe used. Generally, dishes cooked on low will take about 6-8 hours, while those cooked on high may be ready in about 3-4 hours. This flexibility allows users to plan their cooking around their schedules, making it easy to have a delicious meal waiting when they return home.

Understanding the differences between the two settings can help you achieve the best results for your recipes. If you're in a hurry, using the high setting can get your meal ready more quickly, but keep in mind that many recipes yield better results when cooked on low for longer periods. This knowledge can help you make informed decisions about meal prep, ensuring that you enjoy the flavors and textures of your dishes to the fullest.

Lid: It's crucial to keep the lid on during cooking to maintain temperature and moisture. Removing the lid can significantly extend cooking time, as it lets out heat and steam. The design of the Crock Pot features a tightly fitting lid that helps trap moisture, ensuring that your dishes remain juicy and flavorful throughout the cooking process. Keeping the lid on also helps preserve the aromas, creating a more enjoyable cooking experience and allowing you to savor the enticing smells as your meal cooks.

Furthermore, using the lid prevents the need for constant checking, allowing you to focus on other tasks or simply relax while your meal is cooking. The ability to cook without needing to hover over the stove or oven makes the Crock Pot a convenient option for home cooks who appreciate a more laid-back approach to meal preparation.

Serving: Once the cooking time is complete, carefully remove the lid and serve your meal directly from the pot. Many Crock Pots are designed to be visually appealing, making them attractive enough to place on the dining table. This not only simplifies serving but also adds a rustic touch to your dining experience. The ability to serve straight from the pot means fewer dishes to wash, contributing to the overall convenience of using a Crock Pot for meal preparation.

When serving, be mindful of portion sizes, as the slow cooking process often yields generous servings. Consider using a ladle or serving spoon to scoop out portions, and offer sides like crusty bread, rice, or salad to complement your meal. The act of sharing a hearty, home-cooked dish from the Crock Pot fosters a sense of warmth and togetherness at the dinner table.

TIPS FOR USING THE CROCK POT

Ingredient Preparation: Before adding ingredients to your Crock Pot, it's essential to prep them properly. Chop vegetables into uniform sizes to ensure even cooking, and brown meats in a skillet beforehand for added flavor. While browning is optional, it can enhance the taste and texture of your dish, creating a richer flavor profile. For example, searing meats helps develop a caramelized crust that adds depth to your meal.

Additionally, consider using fresh, seasonal ingredients to maximize flavor and nutrition. When selecting produce, look for vibrant colors and firm textures, which are indicators of freshness. Using high-quality ingredients will elevate your dishes and make your meals more enjoyable.

Adjust Cooking Times: Every Crock Pot model can vary slightly in temperature and cooking times, so it's essential to monitor your meals and adjust cooking times as needed. For first-time recipes, check the food towards the end of the suggested cooking time to ensure it's cooked to your liking. If necessary, you can extend cooking times for tougher cuts of meat or heartier vegetables, which benefit from longer cooking periods.

Using a meat thermometer can also help determine doneness, especially for larger cuts of meat. This simple tool ensures that your meals are safe to eat while preventing overcooking, which can lead to dryness and diminished flavor.

Layering Ingredients: Layering is crucial for achieving the best results in a Crock Pot. Place tougher ingredients, like root vegetables, at the bottom of the pot, followed by meats, and finally, more delicate items on top. This order allows for optimal cooking, ensuring that everything is cooked evenly and at the right time. Moreover, the layering technique helps create a steaming effect that enhances moisture retention, resulting in tender, flavorful dishes.

Avoid Overfilling: It's vital not to overfill your Crock Pot, as this can lead to uneven cooking and spills during the cooking process. Most models have a fill line indicating the maximum capacity, so be sure to follow this guideline. Generally, filling the pot about two-thirds full is a good rule of thumb to allow for proper heat circulation. Overfilling can also hinder the cooking process, leading to longer cook times or undercooked ingredients.

Experiment with Recipes: The Crock Pot is an incredibly versatile appliance, and there are countless recipes available online and in cookbooks. Don't be afraid to experiment with new flavors and cuisines, adapting recipes to suit your preferences. The more you use your Crock Pot, the more comfortable you will become with its capabilities, and you may discover unique combinations that become family favorites.

Trying out international dishes, seasonal ingredients, or even desserts in your Crock Pot can be a fun way to expand your cooking repertoire. Enjoy the process of discovery as you explore the possibilities that this appliance offers, making meal preparation an exciting adventure rather than a chore.

CLEANING AND MAINTENANCE

Maintaining your Crock Pot is essential for ensuring its longevity and optimal performance, as well as for preserving the quality of the meals you prepare. After cooking, it's vital to let the appliance cool down completely before starting the cleaning process. This cooling period is important for safety, as the inner ceramic or porcelain pot can retain heat for quite some time after the cooking has stopped. Once the appliance has cooled sufficiently, carefully remove the inner pot from the outer housing and wash it with warm, soapy water. Many inner pots are dishwasher-safe, which can greatly simplify the cleaning process, making it easy to remove stubborn food residues and stains.

In situations where food has become stuck to the pot, soaking it in warm water for a while can help loosen any stubborn debris, making it easier to clean. Pay close attention to the lid, as condensation can accumulate during cooking, leading to potential residue buildup. Wipe down the lid and any steam vent thoroughly with a damp cloth or sponge to ensure all remnants are removed. Regular cleaning not only maintains the appliance's appearance but also prevents flavors from previous meals from transferring to new dishes, ensuring that each culinary creation has its intended taste.

When storing your Crock Pot, make sure it is completely dry to prevent moisture buildup, which can lead to mold or unpleasant odors. Ideally, store the appliance in a cool, dry place, leaving the lid slightly ajar to allow for proper airflow. This practice helps prevent any musty smells and protects the materials from potential damage. Furthermore, take the time to periodically inspect the power cord and heating element for signs of wear, fraying, or damage. If you notice any issues, stop using the appliance immediately and consult the manufacturer's guidelines for repairs or replacements. By prioritizing regular cleaning and maintenance, you not only enhance the performance and reliability of your Crock Pot but also create a more enjoyable cooking experience that allows you to focus on what really matters—creating delicious meals for yourself and your loved ones.

Breakfast Recipes

Leek Bake 12

Ham Pockets 12

Seafood Eggs 12

Carrot Pudding 13

Kale Cups 13

Creamy Yogurt 13

Eggs With Brussel Sprouts 14

Peach Puree 14

Breakfast Meat Rolls 14

Smoked Salmon Omelet 15

Asparagus Egg Casserole 15

Leek Eggs 15

Squash Bowls 16

Broccoli Omelet 16

Sweet Quinoa 16

Chia Oatmeal 17

Bacon Eggs 17

Baby Carrots In Syrup 17

Apricot Butter 18

Chicken Omelet 18

Milk Pudding 18

Olive Eggs 19

Caramel Pecan Sticky Buns 19

Chicken Meatballs 19

Breakfast Recipes

Leek Bake

Servings:3

Cooking Time: 8 Hours

Ingredients:

- 2 cups leek, chopped
- 3 oz Cheddar cheese, shredded
- ¼ cup ground chicken
- 1 teaspoon dried thyme
- ½ cup chicken stock

Directions:

1. Pour the chicken stock in the Crock Pot.
2. Put the leek in the chicken stock and sprinkle it with dried thyme and ground chicken.
3. Then top the chicken with Cheddar cheese and close the lid.
4. Cook the leek bake on low for 8 hours.

Nutrition Info:

- Per Serving: 175 calories, 11.5g protein, 9.1g carbohydrates, 10.6g fat, 1.2g fiber, 40mg cholesterol, 325mg sodium, 168mg potassium.

Ham Pockets

Servings:4

Cooking Time: 1 Hour

Ingredients:

- 4 pita bread
- ½ cup Cheddar cheese, shredded
- 4 ham slices
- 1 tablespoon mayonnaise
- 1 teaspoon dried dill

Directions:

1. Mix cheese with mayonnaise and dill.
2. Then fill the pita bread with sliced ham and cheese mixture.
3. Wrap the stuffed pitas in the foil and place it in the Crock Pot.
4. Cook them on High for 1 hour.

Nutrition Info:

- Per Serving: 283 calories, 13.7g protein, 35.7g carbohydrates, 9.1g fat, 1.7g fiber, 32mg cholesterol, 801mg sodium, 175mg potassium.

Seafood Eggs

Servings:4

Cooking Time: 2.5 Hours

Ingredients:

- 4 eggs, beaten
- 2 tablespoons cream cheese
- 1 teaspoon Italian seasonings
- 6 oz shrimps, peeled
- 1 teaspoon olive oil

Directions:

1. Mix cream cheese with eggs.
2. Add Italian seasonings and shrimps.
3. Then brush the ramekins with olive oil and pour the egg mixture inside.
4. Transfer the ramekins in the Crock Pot.
5. Cook the eggs on High for 2.5 hours.

Nutrition Info:

- Per Serving: 144 calories, 15.6g protein, 1.3g carbohydrates, 8.4g fat, 0g fiber, 260mg cholesterol, 181mg sodium, 138mg potassium

Carrot Pudding

Servings:4

Cooking Time: 5 Hours

Ingredients:

- 3 cups carrot, shredded
- 1 tablespoon potato starch
- 3 tablespoons maple syrup
- 1 teaspoon ground cinnamon
- 4 cups of milk

Directions:

1. Mix potato starch with milk and pour the liquid in the Crock Pot.
2. Add ground cinnamon, maple syrup, and carrot.
3. Close the lid and cook the pudding on Low for 5 hours.

Nutrition Info:

- Per Serving: 206 calories, 8.7g protein, 33.1g carbohydrates, 5g fat, 2.3g fiber, 20mg cholesterol, 173mg sodium, 437mg potassium

Kale Cups

Servings:4

Cooking Time: 2.5 Hours

Ingredients:

- 1 cup kale, chopped
- 4 eggs, beaten
- 1 teaspoon olive oil
- 1 teaspoon chili powder
- ½ cup Cheddar cheese, shredded

Directions:

1. Mix kale with eggs, olive oil, and chili powder.
2. Transfer the mixture in the ramekins and top with Cheddar cheese.

3. Place the ramekins in the Crock Pot.
4. Close the lid and cook the meal on high for 2.5 hours.

Nutrition Info:

- Per Serving: 140 calories, 9.6g protein, 2.6g carbohydrates, 10.3g fat, 0.5g fiber, 179mg cholesterol, 163mg sodium, 168mg potassium

Creamy Yogurt

Servings: 8

Cooking Time: 10 Hours

Ingredients:

- 3 teaspoons gelatin
- ½ gallon milk
- 7 ounces plain yogurt
- 1 and ½ tablespoons vanilla extract
- ½ cup maple syrup

Directions:

1. Put the milk in your Crock Pot, cover and cook on Low for 3 hours.
2. In a bowl, mix 1 cup of hot milk from the Crock Pot with the gelatin, whisk well, pour into the Crock Pot, cover and leave aside for 2 hours.
3. Combine 1 cup of milk with the yogurt, whisk really well and pour into the pot.
4. Also add vanilla and maple syrup, stir, cover and cook on Low for 7 more hours.
5. Leave yogurt aside to cool down and serve it for breakfast.

Nutrition Info:

- calories 200, fat 4, fiber 5, carbs 10, protein 5

Eggs With Brussel Sprouts

Servings: 4

Cooking Time: 6 Hours

Ingredients:

- 1 cup Brussel sprouts, halved
- ½ cup Mozzarella, shredded
- 5 eggs, beaten
- 1 teaspoon chili powder
- 1 teaspoon olive oil

Directions:

1. Pour olive oil in the Crock Pot.
2. Then add the layer of the Brussel sprouts.
3. Sprinkle the vegetables with chili powder and eggs.
4. Then add mozzarella and close the lid.
5. Cook the meal on Low for 6 hours.

Nutrition Info:

- Per Serving: 110 calories, 8.8g protein, 2.9g carbohydrates, 7.5g fat, 1.1g fiber, 206mg cholesterol, 110mg sodium, 172mg potassium

Peach Puree

Servings: 2

Cooking Time: 7 Hours

Ingredients:

- 2 cups peaches, chopped
- 1 tablespoon sugar
- 1 teaspoon ground cinnamon
- ¼ cup of water

Directions:

1. Put all ingredients in the Crock Pot.
2. Close the lid and cook them on low for 7 hours.
3. Then make the puree with the help of the immersion blender.

4. Store the puree in the fridge for up to 1 day.

Nutrition Info:

- Per Serving: 84 calories, 1.5g protein, 20.9g carbohydrates, 0.4g fat, 2.9g fiber, 0mg cholesterol, 1mg sodium, 290mg potassium

Breakfast Meat Rolls

Servings: 12

Cooking Time: 4.5 Hours

Ingredients:

- 1-pound puff pastry
- 1 cup ground pork
- 1 tablespoon garlic, diced
- 1 egg, beaten
- 1 tablespoon sesame oil

Directions:

1. Roll up the puff pastry.
2. Then mix ground pork with garlic and egg.
3. Then spread the puff pastry with ground meat mixture and roll.
4. Cut the puff pastry rolls on small rolls.
5. Then sprinkle the rolls with sesame oil.
6. Arrange the meat rolls in the Crock Pot and close the lid.
7. Cook breakfast on High for 4.5 hours.

Nutrition Info:

- Per Serving: 244 calories, 4.9g protein, 17.3g carbohydrates, 17.2g fat, 0.6g fiber, 20mg cholesterol, 106mg sodium, 31mg potassium.

Smoked Salmon Omelet

Servings:4

Cooking Time: 2 Hours

Ingredients:

- 4 oz smoked salmon, sliced
- 5 eggs, beaten
- 1 teaspoon ground coriander
- 1 teaspoon butter, melted

Directions:

1. Brush the Crock Pot bottom with melted butter.
2. Then mix eggs with ground coriander and pour the liquid in the Crock Pot.
3. Add smoked salmon and close the lid.
4. Cook the omelet on High for 2 hours.

Nutrition Info:

- Per Serving: 120 calories, 12.1g protein, 0.4g carbohydrates, 7.7g fat, 0g fiber, 214mg cholesterol, 651mg sodium, 124mg potassium

Asparagus Egg Casserole

Servings:4

Cooking Time: 2.5 Hours

Ingredients:

- 7 eggs, beaten
- 4 oz asparagus, chopped, boiled
- 1 oz Parmesan, grated
- 1 teaspoon sesame oil
- 1 teaspoon dried dill

Directions:

1. Pour the sesame oil in the Crock Pot.
2. Then mix dried dill with parmesan, asparagus, and eggs.
3. Pour the egg mixture in the Crock Pot and close the lid.

4. Cook the casserole on high for 2.5 hours.

Nutrition Info:

- Per Serving: 149 calories, 12.6g protein, 2.1g carbohydrates, 10.3g fat, 0.6g fiber, 292mg cholesterol, 175mg sodium, 169mg potassium

Leek Eggs

Servings:4

Cooking Time: 2.5 Hours

Ingredients:

- 10 oz leek, sliced
- 4 eggs, beaten
- 1 teaspoon olive oil
- ½ teaspoon cumin seeds
- 3 oz Cheddar cheese, shredded

Directions:

1. Mix leek with olive oil and eggs.
2. Then transfer the mixture in the Crock Pot.
3. Sprinkle the egg mixture with Cheddar cheese and cumin seeds.
4. Close the lid and cook the meal on High for 2.5 hours.

Nutrition Info:

- Per Serving: 203 calories, 11.9g protein, 10.8g carbohydrates, 12.9g fat, 1.3g fiber, 186mg cholesterol, 208mg sodium, 212mg potassium

Squash Bowls

Servings: 2

Cooking Time: 6 Hours

Ingredients:

- 2 tablespoons walnuts, chopped
- 2 cups squash, peeled and cubed
- ½ cup coconut cream
- ½ teaspoon cinnamon powder
- ½ tablespoon sugar

Directions:

1. In your Crock Pot, mix the squash with the nuts and the other ingredients, toss, put the lid on and cook on Low for 6 hours.
2. Divide into bowls and serve.

Nutrition Info:

- calories 140, fat 1, fiber 2, carbs 2, protein 5

Broccoli Omelet

Servings:4

Cooking Time: 2 Hours

Ingredients:

- 5 eggs, beaten
- 1 tablespoon cream cheese
- 3 oz broccoli, chopped
- 1 tomato, chopped
- 1 teaspoon avocado oil

Directions:

1. Mix eggs with cream cheese and transfer in the Crock Pot.
2. Add avocado oil, broccoli, and tomato.
3. Close the lid and cook the omelet on High for 2 hours.

Nutrition Info:

- Per Serving: 99 calories, 7.9g protein, 2.6g

carbohydrates, 6.6g fat, 0.8g fiber, 207mg cholesterol, 92mg sodium, 184mg potassium.

Sweet Quinoa

Servings:4

Cooking Time: 3 Hours

Ingredients:

- 1 cup quinoa
- ¼ cup dates, chopped
- 3 cups of water
- 1 apricot, chopped
- ½ teaspoon ground nutmeg

Directions:

1. Put quinoa, dates, and apricot in the Crock Pot.
2. Add ground nutmeg and mix the mixture.
3. Cook it on high for 3 hours.

Nutrition Info:

- Per Serving: 194 calories, 6.4g protein, 36.7g carbohydrates, 2.8g fat, 4.1g fiber, 0mg cholesterol, 8g sodium, 338mg potassium.

Chia Oatmeal

Servings: 2

Cooking Time: 8 Hours

Ingredients:

- 2 cups almond milk
- 1 cup steel cut oats
- 2 tablespoons butter, soft
- ½ teaspoon almond extract
- 2 tablespoons chia seeds

Directions:

1. In your Crock Pot, mix the oats with the chia seeds and the other ingredients, toss, put the lid on and cook on Low for 8 hours.
2. Stir the oatmeal one more time, divide into 2 bowls and serve.

Nutrition Info:

- calories 812, fat 71.4, fiber 9.4, carbs 41.1, protein 11

Bacon Eggs

Servings:2

Cooking Time: 2 Hours

Ingredients:

- 2 bacon slices
- 2 eggs, hard-boiled, peeled
- ¼ teaspoon ground black pepper
- 1 teaspoon olive oil
- ½ teaspoon dried thyme

Directions:

1. Sprinkle the bacon with ground black pepper and dried thyme.
2. Then wrap the eggs in the bacon and sprinkle with olive oil.
3. Put the eggs in the Crock Pot and cook on High for 2 hours.

Nutrition Info:

- Per Serving: 187 calories, 12.6g protein, 0.9g carbohydrates, 14.7g fat, 0.2g fiber, 185mg cholesterol, 501mg sodium, 172mg potassium.

Baby Carrots In Syrup

Servings:5

Cooking Time: 7 Hours

Ingredients:

- 3 cups baby carrots
- 1 cup apple juice
- 2 tablespoons brown sugar
- 1 teaspoon vanilla extract

Directions:

1. Mix apple juice, brown sugar, and vanilla extract.
2. Pour the liquid in the Crock Pot.
3. Add baby carrots and close the lid.
4. Cook the meal on Low for 7 hours.

Nutrition Info:

- Per Serving: 81 calories, 0g protein, 18.8g carbohydrates, 0.1g fat, 3.7g fiber, 0mg cholesterol, 363mg sodium, 56mg potassium.

Apricot Butter

Servings: 4

Cooking Time: 7 Hours

Ingredients:

- 1 cup apricots, pitted, chopped
- 3 tablespoons butter
- 1 teaspoon ground cinnamon
- 1 teaspoon brown sugar

Directions:

1. Put all ingredients in the Crock Pot and stir well
2. Close the lid and cook them on Low for 7 hours.
3. Then blend the mixture with the help of the immersion blender and cool until cold.

Nutrition Info:

- Per Serving: 99 calories, 0.6g protein, 5.5g carbohydrates, 8.9g fat, 1.1g fiber, 23mg cholesterol, 62mg sodium, 106mg potassium.

Chicken Omelet

Servings: 4

Cooking Time: 3 Hours

Ingredients:

- 4 oz chicken fillet, boiled, shredded
- 1 tomato, chopped
- 4 eggs, beaten
- 1 tablespoon cream cheese
- 1 teaspoon olive oil

Directions:

1. Brush the Crock Pot bowl with olive oil from inside.
2. In the mixing bowl mix shredded chicken, tomato, eggs, and cream cheese.
3. Then pour the mixture in the Crock Pot bowl and close the lid.
4. Cook the omelet for 3 hours on Low.

Nutrition Info:

- Per Serving: 138 calories, 14.1g protein, 1g carbohydrates, 8.5g fat, 0.2g fiber, 192mg cholesterol, 94mg sodium, 168mg potassium.

Milk Pudding

Servings: 2

Cooking Time: 7 Hours

Ingredients:

- 1 cup milk
- 3 eggs, beaten
- 2 tablespoons cornstarch
- 1 teaspoon vanilla extract
- 1 tablespoon white sugar

Directions:

1. Mix milk with eggs and cornstarch.
2. Whisk the mixture until smooth and add vanilla extract and white sugar.
3. Pour the liquid in the Crock Pot and close the lid.
4. Cook it on Low for 7 hours.

Nutrition Info:

- Per Serving: 214 calories, 12.3g protein, 20.1g carbohydrates, 9.1g fat, 9.7g fiber, 0.1mg cholesterol, 151mg sodium, 162mg potassium.

Olive Eggs

Servings: 4

Cooking Time: 2 Hours

Ingredients:

- 10 kalamata olives, sliced
- 8 eggs, beaten
- 1 teaspoon cayenne pepper
- 1 tablespoon butter

Directions:

1. Grease the Crock Pot bottom with butter.
2. Then add beaten eggs and cayenne pepper.
3. After this, top the eggs with olives and close the lid.
4. Cook the eggs on High for 2 hours.

Nutrition Info:

- Per Serving: 165 calories, 11.2g protein, 1.6g carbohydrates, 12.9g fat, 0.5g fiber, 335mg cholesterol, 240mg sodium, 129mg potassium

Caramel Pecan Sticky Buns

Servings: 4

Cooking Time: 2 Hours 40 Minutes

Ingredients:

- ¾ cup packed brown sugar
- 15 ounces refrigerated biscuits
- 1 teaspoon ground cinnamon
- 6 tablespoons melted butter
- ¼ cup pecans, finely chopped

Directions:

1. Mix together brown sugar, cinnamon and chopped nuts in a bowl.
2. Dip refrigerator biscuits in melted butter to coat, then in the brown sugar mixture.
3. Grease a crockpot and layer the biscuits in the crock pot.

4. Top with the remaining brown sugar mixture and cover the lid.
5. Cook on HIGH for about 2 hours and dish out to serve.

Nutrition Info:

- Calories: 583 Fat: 23.5g Carbohydrates: 86.2g

Chicken Meatballs

Servings: 4

Cooking Time: 4 Hours

Ingredients:

- 3 tablespoons bread crumbs
- 1 teaspoon cream cheese
- 10 oz ground chicken
- 1 tablespoon coconut oil
- 1 teaspoon Italian seasonings

Directions:

1. Mix bread crumbs with cream cheese, ground chicken, and Italian seasonings.
2. Make the meatballs and put them in the Crock Pot.
3. Add coconut oil and close the lid.
4. Cook the chicken meatballs for 4 hours on High.

Nutrition Info:

- Per Serving: 190 calories, 21.2g protein, 3.8g carbohydrates, 9.6g fat, 0.2g fiber, 65mg cholesterol, 101mg sodium, 184mg potassium.

Lunch & Dinner Recipes

Blue Cheese Chicken 21

Sweet Farro 21

Cumin Rice 21

Apricot Glazed Gammon 22

Mango Chutney Pork Chops.................22

Asparagus Casserole 22

Coffee Beef Roast 22

Cherry Rice 23

French Onion Sandwich Filling.............23

Beans-rice Mix....................................23

Green Enchilada Pork Roast 24

Sweet Popcorn 24

Butter Buckwheat................................24

Crock Pot Steamed Rice 25

Milky Semolina....................................25

Cauliflower Mashed Potatoes 25

Cider Braised Chicken..........................25

Creamy Polenta....................................26

Salted Caramel Rice Pudding 26

Apple Cups..26

Red Salsa Chicken 27

Beans And Peas Bowl 27

Chicken Drumsticks And Buffalo Sauce..27

Tomato Soy Glazed Chicken 28

Creamed Sweet Corn 28

Lunch & Dinner Recipes

Blue Cheese Chicken

Servings: 4

Cooking Time: 2 1/4 Hours

Ingredients:

- 4 chicken breasts
- 1 teaspoon dried oregano
- Salt and pepper to taste
- 1/2 cup crumbled blue cheese
- 1/2 cup chicken stock

Directions:

1. Season the chicken with salt and pepper and place it in your crock pot.
2. Add the stock then top each piece of chicken with crumbled feta cheese.
3. Cook on high settings for 2 hours.
4. Serve the chicken warm.

Sweet Farro

Servings:3

Cooking Time: 6 Hours

Ingredients:

- ½ cup farro
- 2 cups of water
- ½ cup heavy cream
- 2 tablespoons dried cranberries
- 2 tablespoons sugar

Directions:

1. Chop the cranberries and put in the Crock Pot.
2. Add water, heavy cream, sugar, and farro.
3. Mix the ingredients with the help of the spoon and close the lid.
4. Cook the farro on low for 6 hours.

Nutrition Info:

- Per Serving: 208 calories, 5.1g protein, 31g carbohydrates, 7.4g fat, 2.2g fiber, 27mg cholesterol, 32mg sodium, 24mg potassium.

Cumin Rice

Servings:6

Cooking Time: 3.5 Hours

Ingredients:

- 2 cups long-grain rice
- 5 cups chicken stock
- 1 teaspoon cumin seeds
- 1 teaspoon olive oil
- 1 tablespoon cream cheese

Directions:

1. Heat the olive oil in the skillet.
2. Add cumin seeds and roast them for 2-3 minutes.
3. Then transfer the roasted cumin seeds in the Crock Pot.
4. Add rice and chickens tock. Gently stir the ingredients.
5. Close the lid and cook the rice on high for 3.5 hours.
6. Then add cream cheese and stir the rice well.

Nutrition Info:

- Per Serving: 247 calories, 5.2g protein, 50.1g carbohydrates, 2.3g fat, 0.8g fiber, 2mg cholesterol, 645mg sodium, 91mg potassium.

Apricot Glazed Gammon

Servings: 6-8

Cooking Time: 6 1/4 Hours

Ingredients:

- 3-4 pounds piece of gammon joint
- 1/2 cup apricot preserve
- 1 teaspoon cumin powder
- 1/4 teaspoon chili powder
- 1 cup vegetable stock
- Salt and pepper to taste

Directions:

1. Mix the apricot preserve with cumin powder and chili powder then spread this mixture over the gammon.
2. Place the meat in your Crock Pot and add the stock.
3. Cook on low settings for 6 hours.
4. Serve the gammon with your favorite side dish, warm or chilled.

Mango Chutney Pork Chops

Servings: 4

Cooking Time: 5 1/4 Hours

Ingredients:

- 4 pork chops
- 1 jar mango chutney
- 3/4 cup chicken stock
- 1 bay leaf
- Salt and pepper to taste

Directions:

1. Combine all the ingredients in your crock pot.
2. Add enough salt and pepper and cook on low settings for 5 hours.
3. Serve the pork chops warm.

Asparagus Casserole

Servings: 6

Cooking Time: 6 1/2 Hours

Ingredients:

- 1 bunch asparagus, trimmed and chopped
- 1 can condensed cream of mushroom soup
- 2 hard-boiled eggs, peeled and cubed
- 1 cup grated Cheddar
- 2 cups bread croutons
- Salt and pepper to taste

Directions:

1. Combine the asparagus, mushroom soup, hard-boiled eggs, cheese and bread croutons in your Crock Pot.
2. Add salt and pepper to taste and cook on low settings for 6 hours.
3. Serve the casserole warm and fresh.

Coffee Beef Roast

Servings: 6

Cooking Time: 4 1/4 Hours

Ingredients:

- 2 pounds beef sirloin
- 2 tablespoons olive oil
- 4 garlic cloves, minced
- 1 cup strong brewed coffee
- 1/2 cup beef stock
- Salt and pepper to taste

Directions:

1. Combine all the ingredients in your crock pot, adding salt and pepper to taste.
2. Cover with a lid and cook on high settings for 4 hours.
3. Serve the roast warm and fresh with your favorite side dish.

Cherry Rice

Servings:4

Cooking Time: 3 Hours

Ingredients:

- 1 cup basmati rice
- 1 cup cherries, raw
- 3 cups of water
- 2 tablespoons of liquid honey
- 1 tablespoon butter, melted

Directions:

1. Put cherries and rice in the Crock Pot.
2. Add water and cook the meal on high for 3 hours.
3. Meanwhile, mix liquid honey and butter.
4. When the rice is cooked, add liquid honey mixture and carefully stir.

Nutrition Info:

- Per Serving: 249 calories, 3.9g protein, 51.1g carbohydrates, 3.3g fat, 1.4g fiber, 8mg cholesterol, 29mg sodium, 136mg potassium.

French Onion Sandwich Filling

Servings: 10

Cooking Time: 9 1/4 Hours

Ingredients:

- 4 pounds beef roast
- 4 sweet onions, sliced
- 4 bacon slices, chopped
- 1 teaspoon garlic powder
- 1/2 cup white wine
- Salt and pepper to taste
- 1 thyme sprig

Directions:

1. Combine all the ingredients in your crock pot.
2. Add salt and pepper to taste and cook on low settings for 9 hours.
3. When done, shred the meat into fine threads and use it as sandwich filling, warm or chilled.

Beans-rice Mix

Servings:4

Cooking Time: 3 Hours

Ingredients:

- 5 oz red kidney beans, canned
- 1 teaspoon garlic powder
- ¼ teaspoon ground coriander
- ½ cup long-grain rice
- 2 cups chicken stock

Directions:

1. Put long-grain rice in the Crock Pot.
2. Add chicken stock, ground coriander, and garlic powder.
3. Close the lid and cook the rice for 2.5 hours on High.
4. Then add red kidney beans, stir the mixture, and cook for 30 minutes in High.

Nutrition Info:

- Per Serving: 211 calories, 10.1g protein, 41.1g carbohydrates, 0.8g fat, 5.8g fiber, 0mg cholesterol, 387mg sodium, 523mg potassium.

Green Enchilada Pork Roast

Servings: 8

Cooking Time: 8 1/4 Hours

Ingredients:

- 4 pounds pork roast
- 2 cups green enchilada sauce
- 1/2 cup chopped cilantro
- 2 chipotle peppers, chopped
- 1/2 cup vegetable stock
- Salt and pepper to taste

Directions:

1. Combine the enchilada sauce, cilantro, chipotle peppers and stock in your Crock Pot.
2. Add the pork roast and season with salt and pepper.
3. Cook on low settings for 8 hours.
4. Serve the pork warm with your favorite side dish.

Sweet Popcorn

Servings:4

Cooking Time: 20 Minutes

Ingredients:

- 2 cups popped popcorn
- 2 tablespoons butter
- 2 tablespoons brown sugar
- ½ teaspoon ground cinnamon

Directions:

1. Put butter and sugar in the Crock Pot.
2. Add ground cinnamon and cook the mixture on High or 15 minutes.
3. Then open the lid, stir the mixture, and add popped popcorn.
4. Carefully mix the ingredients with the help of the spatula and cook on high for 5 minutes more.

Nutrition Info:

- Per Serving: 84 calories, 0.6g protein, 7.8g carbohydrates, 5.9g fat, 0.7g fiber, 15mg cholesterol, 43mg sodium, 22mg potassium.

Butter Buckwheat

Servings:4

Cooking Time: 4 Hours

Ingredients:

- 2 tablespoons butter
- 1 cup buckwheat
- 2 cups chicken stock
- ½ teaspoon salt

Directions:

1. Mix buckwheat with salt and transfer in the Crock Pot.
2. Add chicken stock and close the lid.
3. Cook the buckwheat on High for 4 hours.
4. Then add butter, carefully mixture the buckwheat, and transfer in the bowls.

Nutrition Info:

- Per Serving: 202 calories, 6g protein, 30.8g carbohydrates, 7.5g fat, 4.3g fiber, 15mg cholesterol, 714mg sodium, 205mg potassium.

Crock Pot Steamed Rice

Servings: 8

Cooking Time: 4 Hours

Ingredients:

- 2 cups white rice
- 4 cups water
- 1 bay leaf
- Salt and pepper to taste

Directions:

1. Combine all the ingredients in your crock pot.
2. Add salt and pepper as needed and cook on low settings for 4 hours. If possible, stir once during the cooking process.
3. Serve the rice warm or chilled, as a side dish to your favorite veggie main dish.

Milky Semolina

Servings:2

Cooking Time: 1 Hour

Ingredients:

- ¼ cup semolina
- 1 ½ cup milk
- 1 teaspoon vanilla extract
- 1 teaspoon sugar

Directions:

1. Put all ingredients in the Crock Pot.
2. Close the lid and cook the semolina on high for 1 hour.
3. When the meal is cooked, carefully stir it and cool it to room temperature.

Nutrition Info:

- Per Serving: 180 calories, 8.7g protein, 26.5g carbohydrates, 4g fat, 0.8g fiber, 15mg cholesterol, 87mg sodium, 147mg potassium.

Cauliflower Mashed Potatoes

Servings: 4

Cooking Time: 4 1/2 Hours

Ingredients:

- 1 pound potatoes, peeled and cubed
- 2 cups cauliflower florets
- 1/4 cup vegetable stock
- 2 tablespoons coconut oil
- 1/4 cup coconut milk
- Salt and pepper to taste

Directions:

1. Combine the potatoes, cauliflower, stock, coconut oil and coconut milk in your Crock Pot.
2. Add salt and pepper to taste and cook on low settings for 4 hours.
3. When done, mash with a potato masher and serve right away.

Cider Braised Chicken

Servings: 8

Cooking Time: 8 1/4 Hours

Ingredients:

- 1 whole chicken, cut into smaller pieces
- Salt and pepper to taste
- 1 teaspoon dried thyme
- 1 teaspoon dried oregano
- 1 teaspoon cumin powder
- Salt to taste
- 1 1/2 cups apple cider

Directions:

1. Season the chicken with salt, thyme, oregano and cumin powder and place it in your crock pot.
2. Add the apple cider and cook on low settings for 8 hours.
3. Serve the chicken warm with your favorite side dish.

Creamy Polenta

Servings:4

Cooking Time: 2.5 Hours

Ingredients:

- 1 cup polenta
- 3 cups of water
- 1 cup heavy cream
- 1 teaspoon salt

Directions:

1. Put all ingredients in the Crock Pot.
2. Close the lid and cook them on High for 5 hours.
3. When the polenta is cooked, stir it carefully and transfer it in the serving plates.

Nutrition Info:

- Per Serving: 242 calories, 3.5g protein, 31.3g carbohydrates, 11.4g fat, 1g fiber, 41mg cholesterol, 600mg sodium, 24mg potassium.

Salted Caramel Rice Pudding

Servings:2

Cooking Time: 3 Hours

Ingredients:

- 2 teaspoons salted caramel
- ½ cup basmati rice
- 1.5 cup milk
- 1 teaspoon vanilla extract

Directions:

1. Pour milk in the Crock Pot.
2. Add vanilla extract and basmati rice.
3. Cook the rice on high or 3 hours.
4. Then add salted caramel and carefully mix the pudding.
5. Cool it to the room temperature and transfer in the bowls.

Nutrition Info:

- Per Serving: 284 calories, 9.8g protein, 48.9g carbohydrates, 4.7g fat, 0.8g fiber, 16mg cholesterol, 99mg sodium, 161mg potassium.

Apple Cups

Servings:2

Cooking Time: 6 Hours

Ingredients:

- 2 green apples
- 3 oz white rice
- 1 shallot, diced
- ¼ cup of water
- 1 tablespoon cream cheese

Directions:

1. Scoop the flesh from the apples to make the apple cups.
2. Then mix the onion with rice, and curry paste.
3. Pour water in the Crock Pot.
4. Fill the apple cups with rice mixture and top with cream cheese,
5. Then combine the raisins, diced onion, white rice, salt, and curry.
6. Cook the meal on Low for 6 hours.

Nutrition Info:

- Per Serving: 292 calories, 4.1g protein, 65.8g carbohydrates, 2.4g fat, 6g fiber, 6mg cholesterol, 20mg sodium, 310mg potassium.

Red Salsa Chicken

Servings: 8

Cooking Time: 8 1/4 Hours

Ingredients:

- 8 chicken thighs
- 2 cups red salsa
- 1/2 cup chicken stock
- 1 cup grated Cheddar cheese
- Salt and pepper to taste

Directions:

1. Combine the chicken with the salsa and stock in your Crock Pot.
2. Add the cheese and cook on low settings for 8 hours.
3. Serve the chicken warm with your favorite side dish.

Beans And Peas Bowl

Servings:4

Cooking Time: 6 Hours

Ingredients:

- ½ cup black beans, soaked
- 1 cup green peas
- 4 cups of water
- 1 tablespoon tomato paste
- 1 teaspoon sriracha

Directions:

1. Pour water in the Crock Pot.
2. Add black beans and cook them for 5 hours on High.
3. Then add green peas, tomato paste, and sriracha.
4. Stir the ingredients and cook the meal for 1 hour on High.

Nutrition Info:

- Per Serving: 117 calories, 7.4g protein, 21.4g carbohydrates, 0.5g fat, 5.7g fiber, 0mg cholesterol, 23mg sodium, 491mg potassium.

Chicken Drumsticks And Buffalo Sauce

Servings: 2

Cooking Time: 8 Hours

Ingredients:

- 1 pound chicken drumsticks
- 2 tablespoons buffalo wing sauce
- ½ cup chicken stock
- 2 tablespoons honey
- 1 teaspoon lemon juice
- Salt and black pepper to the taste

Directions:

1. In your Crock Pot, mix the chicken with the sauce and the other ingredients, toss, put the lid on and cook on Low for 8 hours.
2. Divide everything between plates and serve.

Nutrition Info:

- calories 361, fat 7, fiber 8, carbs 18, protein 22

Tomato Soy Glazed Chicken

Servings: 8

Cooking Time: 8 1/4 Hours

Ingredients:

- 8 chicken thighs
- 1/2 cup soy sauce
- 2 tablespoons brown sugar
- 1 teaspoon chili powder
- 1/2 cup tomato sauce

Directions:

1. Combine all the ingredients in your crock pot.
2. Cook the chicken on low settings for 8 hours.
3. Serve the chicken warm and fresh.

Creamed Sweet Corn

Servings: 6

Cooking Time: 3 1/4 Hours

Ingredients:

- 2 cans (15 oz.) sweet corn, drained
- 1 cup cream cheese
- 1 cup grated Cheddar cheese
- 1/2 cup heavy cream
- Salt and pepper to taste
- 1 pinch nutmeg

Directions:

1. Combine the corn, cream cheese, Cheddar and cream in your Crock Pot.
2. Add the nutmeg, salt and pepper and cook on low settings for 3 hours.
3. Serve the creamed corn warm.

Beef, Pork & Lamb Recipes

Tender Pork Chops 30	Sweet Beef 34
One Pot Pork Chops 30	Skirt Steak With Red Pepper Sauce 34
Kebab Cubes 30	Roast And Pepperoncinis 34
Chili Beef Sausages 31	Pork Tenderloin And Apples 35
Spiced Beef 31	Pesto Pork Chops 35
Mexican Bubble Pizza 31	Honey Beef Sausages 35
Rosemary Pork 32	Beef Pot Roast 36
Salsa Meat 32	Cheesy Pork Casserole 36
Basil Beef 32	Cajun Beef 36
Crockpot Moroccan Beef 33	Mole Pork Chops 37
Flank Steak With Arugula 33	Soy Beef Steak 37
Stuffed Jalapenos 33	Shredded Pork 37

Beef, Pork & Lamb Recipes

Tender Pork Chops

Servings: 4

Cooking Time: 8 Hours

Ingredients:

- 2 yellow onions, chopped
- 6 bacon slices, chopped
- ½ cup chicken stock
- Salt and black pepper to the taste
- 4 pork chops

Directions:

1. In your Crock Pot, mix onions with bacon, stock, salt, pepper and pork chops, cover and cook on Low for 8 hours.
2. Divide pork chops on plates, drizzle cooking juices all over and serve.

Nutrition Info:

- calories 325, fat 18, fiber 1, carbs 12, protein 36

One Pot Pork Chops

Servings:6

Cooking Time: 10 Hours

Ingredients:

- 6 pork chops
- 2 cups broccoli florets
- ½ cup green and red bell peppers
- 1 onion, sliced
- Salt and pepper to taste

Directions:

1. Place all ingredients in the crockpot.
2. Give a stir to mix everything.
3. Close the lid and cook on low for 10 hours or on high for 8 hours.

Nutrition Info:

- Calories per serving: 496; Carbohydrates: 6g; Protein: 37.1g; Fat: 23.7g; Sugar: 0.8g; Sodium: 563mg; Fiber: 4.3g

Kebab Cubes

Servings:4

Cooking Time: 5 Hours

Ingredients:

- 1 teaspoon curry powder
- 1 teaspoon dried mint
- 1 teaspoon cayenne pepper
- ½ cup plain yogurt
- 1-pound beef tenderloin, cubed

Directions:

1. In the mixing bowl, mix beef cubes with plain yogurt, cayenne pepper, dried mint, and curry powder.
2. Then put the mixture in the Crock Pot. Add water if there is not enough liquid and close the lid.
3. Cook the meal on High for 5 hours.

Nutrition Info:

- Per Serving: 259 calories, 34.7g protein, 2.7g carbohydrates, 10.9g fat, 0.3g fiber, 106mg cholesterol, 89mg sodium, 495mg potassium.

Chili Beef Sausages

Servings:5

Cooking Time: 4 Hours

Ingredients:

- 1-pound beef sausages
- 1 tablespoon olive oil
- ¼ cup of water
- 1 teaspoon chili powder

Directions:

1. Pour olive oil in the Crock Pot.
2. Then sprinkle the beef sausages with chili powder and put in the Crock Pot.
3. Add water and close the lid.
4. Cook the beef sausages on high for 4 hours.

Nutrition Info:

- Per Serving: 385 calories, 12.6g protein, 2.7g carbohydrates, 35.8g fat, 0.2g fiber, 64mg cholesterol, 736mg sodium, 182mg potassium.

Spiced Beef

Servings:4

Cooking Time: 9 Hours

Ingredients:

- 1-pound beef loin
- 1 teaspoon allspice
- 1 teaspoon olive oil
- 1 tablespoon minced onion
- 1 cup of water

Directions:

1. Rub the beef loin with allspice, olive oil, and minced onion.
2. Put the meat in the Crock Pot.
3. Add water and close the lid.
4. Cook the beef on Low for 9 hours.
5. When the meat is cooked, slice it into servings.

Nutrition Info:

- Per Serving: 219 calories, 30.4g protein, 0.6g carbohydrates, 10.7g fat, 0.2g fiber, 81mg cholesterol, 65mg sodium, 395mg potassium.

Mexican Bubble Pizza

Servings:6

Cooking Time: 6 Hours

Ingredients:

- 1 ½ pound ground beef
- 1 tablespoon taco seasoning
- 2 cups cheddar cheese, shredded
- 1 cup mozzarella cheese
- 1 can condensed tomato soup

Directions:

1. Heat skillet over medium flame and brown the ground beef for a few minutes. Stir in taco seasoning.
2. Place the cheddar cheese into the crockpot.
3. Add the sautéed ground beef on top of the cheddar cheese.
4. Pour the tomato sauce.
5. Sprinkle with mozzarella cheese on top.
6. Close the lid and cook on low for 6 hours and on high for 4 hours.

Nutrition Info:

- Calories per serving: 643; Carbohydrates: 5g; Protein: 45g; Fat: 35g; Sugar:2.1 g; Sodium: 1870mg; Fiber: 2.6g

Rosemary Pork

Servings: 4

Cooking Time: 7 Hours

Ingredients:

- 4 pork chops, bone in
- 1 cup chicken stock
- Salt and black pepper to the taste
- 1 teaspoon rosemary, dried
- 3 garlic cloves, minced

Directions:

1. Season pork chops with salt and pepper and place in your Crock Pot.
2. Add rosemary, garlic and stock, cover and cook on Low for 7 hours.
3. Divide pork between plates and drizzle cooking juices all over.

Nutrition Info:

- calories 165, fat 2, fiber 1, carbs 12, protein 26

Salsa Meat

Servings:4

Cooking Time: 4 Hours

Ingredients:

- 1-pound pork sirloin, sliced
- 1 cup tomatillo salsa
- 2 garlic cloves, diced
- 1 teaspoon apple cider vinegar
- ½ cup of water

Directions:

1. Put all ingredients in the Crock Pot and carefully mix.
2. Then close the lid and cook the salsa meat on high for 4 hours.

Nutrition Info:

- Per Serving: 214 calories, 23.8g protein, 2.3g carbohydrates, 11.2g fat, 0.4g fiber, 71mg cholesterol, 169mg sodium, 75mg potassium

Basil Beef

Servings:4

Cooking Time: 4 Hours

Ingredients:

- 1-pound beef loin, chopped
- 2 tablespoons dried basil
- 2 tablespoons butter
- ½ cup of water
- 1 teaspoon salt

Directions:

1. Toss the butter in the skillet and melt it.
2. Then mix the beef loin with dried basil and put in the hot butter.
3. Roast the meat for 2 minutes per side and transfer in the Crock Pot.
4. Add salt and water.
5. Close the lid and cook the beef on high for 4 hours.

Nutrition Info:

- Per Serving: 220 calories, 21g protein, 1.4g carbohydrates, 13.9g fat, 0g fiber, 76mg cholesterol, 1123mg sodium, 6mg potassium.

Crockpot Moroccan Beef

Servings:8

Cooking Time: 10 Hours

Ingredients:

- 2 pounds beef roast, cut into strips
- ½ cup onions, sliced
- 4 tablespoons garam masala
- 1 teaspoon salt
- ½ cup bone broth

Directions:

1. Place all ingredients in the CrockPot.
2. Give a good stir.
3. Close the lid and cook on high for 8 hours or on low for 10 hours.

Nutrition Info:

- Calories per serving: 310; Carbohydrates: 0.7g; Protein: 30.3g; Fat: 25.5g; Sugar: 0g; Sodium: 682mg; Fiber: 0.5g

Flank Steak With Arugula

Servings:4

Cooking Time: 10 Hours

Ingredients:

- 1-pound flank steak
- 1 teaspoon Worcestershire sauce
- Salt and pepper to taste
- 1 package arugula salad mix
- 2 tablespoon balsamic vinegar

Directions:

1. Season the flank steak with Worcestershire sauce, salt, and pepper.
2. Place in the crockpot that has been lined with aluminum foil.
3. Close the lid and cook on low for 10 hours or on high for 7 hours.

4. Meanwhile, prepare the salad by combining the arugula salad mix and balsamic vinegar. Set aside in the fridge.
5. Once the steak is cooked, allow to cool before slicing.
6. Serve on top of the arugula salad.

Nutrition Info:

- Calories per serving: 452; Carbohydrates: 5.8g; Protein: 30.2g; Fat:29.5g; Sugar: 1.2g; Sodium: 563mg; Fiber:3 g

Stuffed Jalapenos

Servings:3

Cooking Time: 4.5 Hours

Ingredients:

- 6 jalapenos, deseed
- 4 oz minced beef
- 1 teaspoon garlic powder
- ½ cup of water

Directions:

1. Mix the minced beef with garlic powder.
2. Then fill the jalapenos with minced meat and arrange it in the Crock Pot.
3. Add water and cook the jalapenos on High for 4.5 hours.

Nutrition Info:

- Per Serving: 55 calories, 7.5g protein, 2.3g carbohydrates, 1.9g fat, 0.9g fiber, 0mg cholesterol, 2mg sodium, 71mg potassium.

Sweet Beef

Servings:4

Cooking Time: 5 Hours

Ingredients:

- 1-pound beef roast, sliced
- 1 tablespoon maple syrup
- 2 tablespoons lemon juice
- 1 teaspoon dried oregano
- 1 cup of water

Directions:

1. Mix water with maple syrup, lemon juice, and dried oregano.
2. Then pour the liquid in the Crock Pot.
3. Add beef roast and close the lid.
4. Cook the meal on High for 5 hours.

Nutrition Info:

- Per Serving: 227 calories, 34.5g protein, 3.8g carbohydrates, 7.2g fat, 0.2g fiber, 101mg cholesterol, 78mg sodium, 483mg potassium.

Skirt Steak With Red Pepper Sauce

Servings:4

Cooking Time: 12 Hours

Ingredients:

- 2 red bell peppers, chopped
- 2 tablespoons olive oil
- 1 teaspoon thyme leaves
- 1-pound skirt steak, sliced into 1 inch thick
- Salt and pepper to taste

Directions:

1. In a food processor, mix together the red bell peppers, olive oil, and thyme leaves. Blend until smooth. Add water to make the mixture slightly runny. Set aside.

2. Season the skirt steak with salt and pepper.
3. Place in the crockpot and pour over the pepper sauce.
4. Add more salt and pepper if desired.
5. Close the lid and cook on low for 12 hours or on high for 10 hours.

Nutrition Info:

- Calories per serving: 396; Carbohydrates:4 g; Protein: 32.5g; Fat: 21g; Sugar: 0g; Sodium: 428mg; Fiber: 2.8g

Roast And Pepperoncinis

Servings: 4

Cooking Time: 8 Hours

Ingredients:

- 5 pounds beef chuck roast
- 1 tablespoon soy sauce
- 10 pepperoncinis
- 1 cup beef stock
- 2 tablespoons butter, melted

Directions:

1. In your Crock Pot, mix beef roast with soy sauce, pepperoncinis, stock and butter, toss well, cover and cook on Low for 8 hours.
2. Transfer roast to a cutting board, shred using2 forks, return to Crock Pot, toss, divide between plates and serve.

Nutrition Info:

- calories 362, fat 4, fiber 8, carbs 17, protein 17

Pork Tenderloin And Apples

Servings: 4

Cooking Time: 8 Hours

Ingredients:

- A pinch of nutmeg, ground
- 2 pounds pork tenderloin
- 4 apples, cored and sliced
- 2 tablespoons maple syrup

Directions:

1. Place apples in your Crock Pot, sprinkle nutmeg over them, add pork tenderloin, sprinkle some more nutmeg, drizzle the maple syrup, cover and cook on Low for 8 hours.
2. Slice pork tenderloin, divide it between plates and serve with apple slices and cooking juices.

Nutrition Info:

- calories 400, fat 4, fiber 5, carbs 12, protein 20

Pesto Pork Chops

Servings:4

Cooking Time: 8 Hours

Ingredients:

- 4 pork chops
- 4 teaspoons pesto sauce
- 4 tablespoons butter

Directions:

1. Brush pork chops with pesto sauce.
2. Put butter in the Crock Pot.
3. Add pork chops and close the lid.
4. Cook the meat on low for 8 hours.
5. Then transfer the cooked pork chops in the plates and sprinkle with butter-pesto gravy from the Crock Pot.

Nutrition Info:

- Per Serving: 380 calories, 18.6g protein, 0.3g carbohydrates, 33.6g fat, 0.1g fiber, 101mg cholesterol, 89mg sodium, 279mg potassium

Honey Beef Sausages

Servings:4

Cooking Time: 4.5 Hours

Ingredients:

- 1-pound beef sausages
- 2 tablespoons of liquid honey
- 1 teaspoon dried dill
- ½ teaspoon salt
- ¼ cup heavy cream

Directions:

1. In the mixing bowl mix liquid honey with dried dill and salt.
2. Then add cream and whisk until smooth.
3. Pour the liquid in the Crock Pot.
4. Add beef sausages and close the lid.
5. Cook the meal on High for 4.5 hours.

Nutrition Info:

- Per Serving: 507 calories, 15.9g protein, 12.1g carbohydrates, 43.9g fat, 0.1g fiber, 91mg cholesterol, 1207mg sodium, 234mg potassium

Beef Pot Roast

Servings:6

Cooking Time: 12 Hours

Ingredients:

- 2 pounds shoulder pot roast, bones removed
- Salt and pepper to taste
- ¼ cup water
- 1 package mushrooms, sliced
- 1 tablespoon Worcestershire sauce

Directions:

1. Place all ingredients in the crockpot.
2. Give a good stir.
3. Close the lid and cook on low for 12 hours or on high for 10 hours.

Nutrition Info:

- Calories per serving: 419; Carbohydrates:3 g; Protein: 32.6g; Fat: 29.6g; Sugar: 0.7g; Sodium: 513mg; Fiber: 1.4g

Cheesy Pork Casserole

Servings:4

Cooking Time: 10 Hours

Ingredients:

- 4 pork chops, bones removed and sliced
- 1 cauliflower head, cut into florets
- 1 cup chicken broth
- 1 teaspoon rosemary
- 2 cups cheddar cheese

Directions:

1. Arrange the pork chop slices in the crockpot,
2. Add in the cauliflower florets.
3. Pour the chicken broth and rosemary. Season with salt and pepper to taste.
4. Pour cheddar cheese on top.
5. Close the lid and cook on low for 10 hours.

Nutrition Info:

- Calories per serving: 417; Carbohydrates: 7g; Protein: 32.1g; Fat: 26.2g; Sugar: 0; Sodium: 846mg; Fiber: 5.3g

Cajun Beef

Servings:4

Cooking Time: 5 Hours

Ingredients:

- 1-pound beef ribs
- 1 tablespoon Cajun seasonings
- 3 tablespoons lemon juice
- 1 tablespoon coconut oil, melted
- ½ cup of water

Directions:

1. Rub the beef ribs with Cajun seasonings and sprinkle with lemon juice.
2. Then pour the coconut oil in the Crock Pot.
3. Add beef ribs and water.
4. Close the lid and cook the beef on high for 5 hours.

Nutrition Info:

- Per Serving: 243 calories, 34.5g protein, 0.2g carbohydrates, 10.6g fat, 0.1g fiber, 101mg cholesterol, 115mg sodium, 471mg potassium.

Mole Pork Chops

Servings:3

Cooking Time: 10 Hours

Ingredients:

- 1 tablespoon butter, melted
- 3 pork chops, bone in
- 2 teaspoons paprika
- ½ teaspoon cocoa powder, unsweetened
- Salt and pepper to taste

Directions:

1. Place the butter into the crockpot.
2. Season the pork chops with paprika, cocoa powder, salt and pepper.
3. Arrange in the crockpot.
4. Close the lid and cook on low for 10 hours or on high for 8 hours.
5. Halfway through the cooking time, be sure to flip the pork chops.

Nutrition Info:

- Calories per serving: 579; Carbohydrates: 1.2g; Protein: 41.7g; Fat: 34.7g; Sugar: 0g; Sodium: 753mg; Fiber: 0g

Soy Beef Steak

Servings:4

Cooking Time: 12 Hours

Ingredients:

- 2 pounds beef tenderloin, sliced thinly
- ¼ cup soy sauce
- ¼ cup lemon juice
- 1 bay leaf
- 1 large red onion, sliced into rings

Directions:

1. Place all ingredients in the crockpot.
2. Give a good stir.

3. Close the lid and cook on low for 12 hours or on high for 10 hours.

Nutrition Info:

- Calories per serving:362; Carbohydrates: 3g; Protein: 23.8g; Fat: 15.3g; Sugar: 0g; Sodium: 724mg; Fiber: 2.4g

Shredded Pork

Servings:4

Cooking Time: 5 Hours

Ingredients:

- 10 oz pork loin
- ½ cup cream
- 1 cup of water
- 1 teaspoon coriander seeds
- 1 teaspoon salt

Directions:

1. Put all ingredients in the Crock Pot.
2. Cook it on High for 5 hours.
3. Then open the lid and shredded pork with the help of 2 forks.

Nutrition Info:

- Per Serving: 191 calories, 19.6g protein, 0.9g carbohydrates, 11.5g fat, 0g fiber, 62mg cholesterol, 367mg sodium, 312mg potassium

Poultry Recipes

Lemon Garlic Dump Chicken................39

Garlic Duck..39

Chicken Wings In Vodka Sauce.............39

Chicken Stuffed With Plums..................40

Lemony Chicken.......................................40

Salsa Chicken Wings..............................40

Chicken Masala..41

Rosemary Rotisserie Chicken.................41

Chicken With Basil And Tomatoes.........41

Buffalo Chicken Tenders.........................42

Stuffed Chicken Fillets............................42

Sun-dried Tomato Chicken 42

Asian Sesame Chicken...........................43

Chicken And Green Onion Sauce 43

Wine Chicken...43

Halved Chicken..44

Mediterranean Stuffed Chicken 44

Horseradish Chicken Wings....................44

Bacon Chicken Wings.............................45

Garlic Pulled Chicken.............................45

Chicken Provolone...................................45

Easy Chicken Continental......................46

Tender Duck Fillets.................................46

Turkey With Plums 46

Poultry Recipes

Lemon Garlic Dump Chicken

Servings:6

Cooking Time: 8 Hours

Ingredients:

- ¼ cup olive oil
- 2 teaspoon garlic, minced
- 6 chicken breasts, bones removed
- 1 tablespoon parsley, chopped
- 2 tablespoons lemon juice, freshly squeezed

Directions:

1. Heat oil in a skillet over medium flame.
2. Sauté the garlic until golden brown.
3. Arrange the chicken breasts in the crockpot.
4. Pour over the oil with garlic.
5. Add the parsley and lemon juice. Add a little water.
6. Close the lid and cook on low for 8 hours or on high for 6 hours.

Nutrition Info:

- Calories per serving: 581; Carbohydrates: 0.7g; Protein: 60.5g; Fat: 35.8g; Sugar: 0g; Sodium: 583mg; Fiber: 0.3g

Garlic Duck

Servings:4

Cooking Time: 5 Hours

Ingredients:

- 1-pound duck fillet
- 1 tablespoon minced garlic
- 1 tablespoon butter, softened
- 1 teaspoon dried thyme
- 1/3 cup coconut cream

Directions:

1. Mix minced garlic with butter, and dried thyme.
2. Then rub the suck fillet with garlic mixture and place it in the Crock Pot.
3. Add coconut cream and cook the duck on High for 5 hours.
4. Then slice the cooked duck fillet and sprinkle it with hot garlic coconut milk.

Nutrition Info:

- Per Serving: 216 calories, 34.1g protein, 2g carbohydrates, 8.4g fat, 0.6g fiber, 8mg cholesterol, 194mg sodium, 135mg potassium.

Chicken Wings In Vodka Sauce

Servings:4

Cooking Time: 6 Hours

Ingredients:

- 1-pound chicken wings
- ½ cup vodka sauce
- 1 tablespoon olive oil

Directions:

1. Put all ingredients in the Crock Pot and mix well.
2. Close the lid and cook the meal on Low for 6 hours.

Nutrition Info:

- Per Serving: 273 calories, 34.1g protein, 2.8g carbohydrates, 13.2g fat, 0g fiber, 102mg cholesterol, 208mg sodium, 276mg potassium.

Chicken Stuffed With Plums

Servings: 6

Cooking Time: 4 Hours

Ingredients:

- 6 chicken fillets
- 1 cup plums, pitted, sliced
- 1 cup of water
- 1 teaspoon salt
- 1 teaspoon white pepper

Directions:

1. Beat the chicken fillets gently and rub with salt and white pepper.
2. Then put the sliced plums on the chicken fillets and roll them.
3. Secure the chicken rolls with toothpicks and put in the Crock Pot.
4. Add water and close the lid.
5. Cook the meal on High for 4 hours.
6. Then remove the chicken from the Crock Pot, remove the toothpicks and transfer in the serving plates.

Nutrition Info:

- Per Serving: 283 calories, 42.4g protein, 1.6g carbohydrates, 10.9g fat, 0.2g fiber, 130mg cholesterol, 514mg sodium, 377mg potassium.

Lemony Chicken

Servings: 6

Cooking Time: 4 Hours

Ingredients:

- 1 whole chicken, cut into medium pieces
- Salt and black pepper to the taste
- Zest of 2 lemons
- Juice of 2 lemons
- Lemon rinds from 2 lemons

Directions:

1. Put chicken pieces in your Crock Pot, season with salt and pepper to the taste, drizzle lemon juice, add lemon zest and lemon rinds, cover and cook on High for 4 hours.
2. Discard lemon rinds, divide chicken between plates, drizzle sauce from the Crock Pot over it and serve.

Nutrition Info:

- calories 334, fat 24, fiber 2, carbs 4.5, protein 27

Salsa Chicken Wings

Servings: 5

Cooking Time: 6 Hours

Ingredients:

- 2-pounds chicken wings
- 2 cups salsa
- ½ cup of water

Directions:

1. Put all ingredients in the Crock Pot.
2. Carefully mix the mixture and close the lid.
3. Cook the chicken wings on low for 6 hours.

Nutrition Info:

- Per Serving: 373 calories, 54.1g protein, 6.5g carbohydrates, 13.6g fat, 1.7g fiber, 161mg cholesterol, 781mg sodium, 750mg potassium.

Chicken Masala

Servings:4

Cooking Time: 4 Hours

Ingredients:

- 1 teaspoon garam masala
- 1 teaspoon ground ginger
- 1 cup of coconut milk
- 1-pound chicken fillet, sliced
- 1 teaspoon olive oil

Directions:

1. Mix coconut milk with ground ginger, garam masala, and olive oil.
2. Add chicken fillet and mix the ingredients.
3. Then transfer them in the Crock Pot and cook on High for 4 hours.

Nutrition Info:

- Per Serving: 365 calories, 34.2g protein, 3.6g carbohydrates, 23.9g fat, 1.4g fiber, 101mg cholesterol, 108mg sodium, 439mg potassium.

Rosemary Rotisserie Chicken

Servings:12

Cooking Time: 12 Hours

Ingredients:

- 1-gallon water
- ¾ cup salt
- ½ cup butter
- 2 tablespoons rosemary and other herbs of your choice
- 1 whole chicken, excess fat removed

Directions:

1. In a pot, combine the water, salt, sugar, and herbs.
2. Stir to dissolve the salt and sugar.
3. Submerge the chicken completely and allow to sit in the brine for 12 hours inside the fridge.
4. Line the crockpot with tin foil.
5. Place the chicken and cook on low for 12 hours or on high for 7 hours.

Nutrition Info:

- Calories per serving: 194; Carbohydrates: 1.4g; Protein:20.6 g; Fat:6.2g; Sugar: 0g; Sodium: 562mg; Fiber: 0.9g

Chicken With Basil And Tomatoes

Servings:4

Cooking Time: 8 Hours

Ingredients:

- ¾ cup balsamic vinegar
- ¼ cup fresh basil leaves
- 2 tablespoons olive oil
- 8 plum tomatoes, sliced
- 4 boneless chicken breasts, bone and skin removed

Directions:

1. Place balsamic vinegar, basil leaves, olive oil and tomatoes in a blender. Season with salt and pepper to taste. Pulse until fine.
2. Arrange the chicken pieces in the crockpot.
3. Pour over the sauce.
4. Close the lid and cook on low for 8 hours or on high for 6 hours.

Nutrition Info:

- Calories per serving: 177; Carbohydrates:4 g; Protein:24 g; Fat: 115g; Sugar: 0g; Sodium: 171mg; Fiber: 3.5g

Buffalo Chicken Tenders

Servings: 4

Cooking Time: 3.5 Hours

Ingredients:

- 12 oz chicken fillet
- 3 tablespoons buffalo sauce
- ½ cup of coconut milk
- 1 jalapeno pepper, chopped

Directions:

1. Cut the chicken fillet into tenders and sprinkle the buffalo sauce.
2. Put the chicken tenders in the Crock Pot.
3. Add coconut milk and jalapeno pepper.
4. Close the lid and cook the meal on high for 3.5 hours.

Nutrition Info:

- Per Serving: 235 calories, 25.3g protein, 2.4g carbohydrates, 13.5g fat, 1g fiber, 76mg cholesterol, 318mg sodium, 293mg potassium.

Stuffed Chicken Fillets

Servings: 6

Cooking Time: 4 Hours

Ingredients:

- ½ cup green peas, cooked
- ½ cup long-grain rice, cooked
- 16 oz chicken fillets
- 1 cup of water
- 1 teaspoon Italian seasonings

Directions:

1. Make the horizontal cuts in chicken fillets.
2. After this, mix Italian seasonings with rice and green peas.
3. Fill the chicken fillet with rice mixture and secure them with toothpicks.
4. Put the chicken fillets in the Crock Pot.
5. Add water and close the lid.
6. Cook the chicken on high for 4 hours.

Nutrition Info:

- Per Serving: 212 calories, 23.6g protein, 14.2g carbohydrates, 6g fat, 0.8g fiber, 68mg cholesterol, 68mg sodium, 232mg potassium.

Sun-dried Tomato Chicken

Servings: 10

Cooking Time: 8 Hours

Ingredients:

- 1 tablespoon butter
- 3 cloves of garlic, minced
- 4 pounds whole chicken, cut into pieces
- 1 cup sun-dried tomatoes in vinaigrette
- Salt and pepper to taste

Directions:

1. In a skillet, melt the butter and sauté the garlic until lightly browned.
2. Add the chicken pieces and cook for 3 minutes until slightly browned.
3. Transfer to the crockpot and stir in the sun-dried tomatoes including the vinaigrette.
4. Season with salt and pepper to taste.
5. Close the lid and cook on low for 8 hours or on high for 6 hours.

Nutrition Info:

- Calories per serving: 397; Carbohydrates:9.4 g; Protein: 30.26g; Fat:14.1 g; Sugar: 0.4g; Sodium: 472mg; Fiber: 5.8g

Asian Sesame Chicken

Servings:12

Cooking Time: 8 Hours

Ingredients:

- 12 chicken thighs, bones and skin removed
- 2 tablespoons sesame oil
- 3 tablespoons water
- 3 tablespoons soy sauce
- 1 thumb-size ginger, sliced thinly

Directions:

1. Place all ingredients in the crockpot.
2. Stir all ingredients to combine.
3. Close the lid and cook on low for 8 hours or on high for 6 hours.
4. Once cooked, garnish with toasted sesame seeds.

Nutrition Info:

- Calories per serving: 458; Carbohydrates: 1.5g; Protein: 32.2g; Fat: 35.05g; Sugar: 0g; Sodium: 426mg; Fiber: 0.4g

Chicken And Green Onion Sauce

Servings: 4

Cooking Time: 4 Hours

Ingredients:

- 2 tablespoons butter, melted
- 4 green onions, chopped
- 4 chicken breast halves, skinless and boneless
- Salt and black pepper to the taste
- 8 ounces sour cream

Directions:

1. In your Crock Pot, mix chicken with melted butter, green onion, salt, pepper and sour cream, cover and cook on High for 4 hours.

2. Divide chicken between plates, drizzle green onions sauce all over and serve.

Nutrition Info:

- calories 200, fat 7, fiber 2, carbs 11, protein 20

Wine Chicken

Servings:4

Cooking Time: 3 Hours

Ingredients:

- 1 cup red wine
- 1-pound chicken breast, skinless, boneless, chopped
- 1 anise star
- 1 teaspoon cayenne pepper
- 2 garlic cloves, crushed

Directions:

1. Pour red wine in the Crock Pot.
2. Add anise star, cayenne pepper, and garlic cloves.
3. Then add chopped chicken and close the lid.
4. Cook the meal on High for 3 hours.
5. Serve the chicken with hot wine sauce.

Nutrition Info:

- Per Serving: 182 calories, 24.2g protein, 2.4g carbohydrates, 2.9g fat, 0.2g fiber, 73mg cholesterol, 61mg sodium, 493mg potassium.

Halved Chicken

Servings:4

Cooking Time: 5 Hours

Ingredients:

- 2-pounds whole chicken, halved
- 1 tablespoon salt
- 1 teaspoon ground black pepper
- 2 tablespoons mayonnaise
- ½ cup of water

Directions:

1. Mix the ground black pepper with salt and mayonnaise.
2. Then rub the chicken halves with mayonnaise mixture and transfer in the Crock Pot.
3. Add water and close the lid.
4. Cook the chicken on High for 5 hours.

Nutrition Info:

- Per Serving: 461 calories, 65.7g protein, 2.1g carbohydrates, 19.3g fat, 1.2g fiber, 0.1mg cholesterol, 1993mg sodium, 559mg potassium.

Mediterranean Stuffed Chicken

Servings:4

Cooking Time: 8 Hours

Ingredients:

- 4 chicken breasts, bones and skin removed
- Salt and pepper to taste
- 1 cup feta cheese, crumbled
- 1/3 cup sun-dried tomatoes, chopped
- 2 tablespoons olive oil

Directions:

1. Create a slit in the chicken breasts to thin out the meat. Season with salt and pepper to taste
2. In a mixing bowl, combine the feta cheese and sun-dried tomatoes.
3. Spoon the feta cheese mixture into the slit created into the chicken.
4. Close the slit using toothpicks.
5. Brush the chicken with olive oil.
6. Place in the crockpot and cook on high for 6 hours or on low for 8 hours.

Nutrition Info:

- Calories per serving: 332; Carbohydrates: 3g; Protein:40 g; Fat: 17g; Sugar: 0g; Sodium: 621mg; Fiber:2.4 g

Horseradish Chicken Wings

Servings:4

Cooking Time: 6 Hours

Ingredients:

- 3 tablespoons horseradish, grated
- 1 teaspoon ketchup
- 1 tablespoon mayonnaise
- ½ cup of water
- 1-pound chicken wings

Directions:

1. Mix chicken wings with ketchup, horseradish, and mayonnaise,
2. Put them in the Crock Pot and add water.
3. Cook the meal on Low for 6 hours.

Nutrition Info:

- Per Serving: 236 calories, 33g protein, 2.5g carbohydrates, 9.7g fat, 0.4g fiber, 102mg cholesterol, 174mg sodium, 309mg potassium.

Bacon Chicken Wings

Servings:4

Cooking Time: 3 Hours

Ingredients:

- 4 chicken wings, boneless
- 4 bacon slices
- 1 tablespoon maple syrup
- ½ teaspoon ground black pepper
- ½ cup of water

Directions:

1. Sprinkle the chicken wings with ground black pepper and maple syrup.
2. Then wrap every chicken wing in the bacon and place it in the Crock Pot.
3. Add water and close the lid.
4. Cook the chicken wings in High for 3 hours.

Nutrition Info:

- Per Serving: 367 calories, 16.1g protein, 25.8g carbohydrates, 22g fat, 1.1g fiber, 41mg cholesterol, 840mg sodium, 121mg potassium.

Garlic Pulled Chicken

Servings:4

Cooking Time: 4 Hours

Ingredients:

- 1-pound chicken breast, skinless, boneless
- 1 tablespoon minced garlic
- 2 cups of water
- ½ cup plain yogurt

Directions:

1. Put the chicken breast in the Crock Pot.
2. Add minced garlic and water.
3. Close the lid and cook the chicken on High for 4 hours.
4. Then drain water and shred the chicken breast.

5. Add plain yogurt and stir the pulled chicken well.

Nutrition Info:

- Per Serving: 154 calories, 25.9g protein, 2.9g carbohydrates, 3.2g fat, 0g fiber, 74mg cholesterol, 83mg sodium, 501mg potassium.

Chicken Provolone

Servings:4

Cooking Time: 8 Hours

Ingredients:

- 4 chicken breasts, bones and skin removed
- Salt and pepper to taste
- 8 fresh basil leaves
- 4 slices prosciutto
- 4 slices provolone cheese

Directions:

1. Sprinkle the chicken breasts with salt and pepper to taste.
2. Place in the crockpot and add the basil leaves, and prosciutto on top.
3. Arrange the provolone cheese slices on top.
4. Close the lid and cook on low for 8 hours and on high for 6 hours.

Nutrition Info:

- Calories per serving: 236; Carbohydrates: 1g; Protein: 33g; Fat: 11g; Sugar:0 g; Sodium: 435mg; Fiber:0 g

Easy Chicken Continental

Servings: 2

Cooking Time: 7 Hours

Ingredients:

- 2 oz dried beef
- 8 oz chicken breast, skinless, boneless, chopped
- ½ cup cream
- ½ can onion soup
- 1 tablespoon cornstarch

Directions:

1. Put 1 oz of the dried beef in the Crock Pot in one layer.
2. Then add chicken breast and top it with remaining dried beef.
3. After this, mix cream cheese, onion, and cornstarch. Whisk the mixture and pour it over the chicken and dried beef.
4. Cook the meal on Low for 7 hours.

Nutrition Info:

- Per Serving: 270 calories, 35.4g protein, 10.5g carbohydrates, 9g fat, 0.6g fiber, 109mg cholesterol, 737mg sodium, 598mg potassium.

Tender Duck Fillets

Servings: 3

Cooking Time: 8 Hours

Ingredients:

- 1 tablespoon butter
- 1 teaspoon dried rosemary
- 1 teaspoon ground nutmeg
- 9 oz duck fillet
- 1 cup of water

Directions:

1. Slice the fillet.

2. Then melt the butter in the skillet.
3. Add sliced duck fillet and roast it for 2-3 minutes per side on medium heat.
4. Transfer the roasted duck fillet and butter in the Crock Pot.
5. Add dried rosemary, ground nutmeg, and water.
6. Close the lid and cook the meal on Low for 8 hours.

Nutrition Info:

- Per Serving: 145 calories, 25.2g protein, 0.6g carbohydrates, 4.7g fat, 0.3g fiber, 10mg cholesterol, 158mg sodium, 61mg potassium.

Turkey With Plums

Servings: 5

Cooking Time: 8 Hours

Ingredients:

- 1-pound turkey fillet, chopped
- 1 cup plums, pitted, halved
- 1 teaspoon ground cinnamon
- 1 cup of water
- 1 teaspoon ground black pepper

Directions:

1. Mix the turkey with ground cinnamon and ground black pepper.
2. Then transfer it in the Crock Pot.
3. Add water and plums.
4. Close the lid and cook the meal on Low for 8 hours.

Nutrition Info:

- Per Serving: 94 calories, 19g protein, 2.2g carbohydrates, 0.5g fat, 0.5g fiber, 47mg cholesterol, 207mg sodium, 29mg potassium.

Fish & Seafood Recipes

Lemony Shrimps In Hoisin Sauce 48

Crab Legs 48

Butter Smelt 48

Ginger Cod 49

Butter Tilapia 49

Butter Salmon 49

Pesto Salmon 50

Soy Sauce Catfish 50

Shrimps Boil 50

Spicy Curried Shrimps 51

Butter Crab 51

Thyme And Sesame Halibut 51

Crockpot Greek Snapper 52

Salmon Stew 52

Chili Salmon 52

Cinnamon Catfish 53

Creamy Pangasius 53

Taco Mahi Mahi 53

Garlic Perch 54

Poached Catfish 54

Mustard Cod 54

Garlic Tuna 55

Scallops With Sour Cream And Dill 55

Spicy Basil Shrimp 55

Fish & Seafood Recipes

Lemony Shrimps In Hoisin Sauce

Servings:4

Cooking Time: 2 Hours

Ingredients:

- 1/3 cup hoisin sauce
- ½ cup lemon juice, freshly squeezed
- 1 ½ pounds shrimps, shelled and deveined
- Salt and pepper to taste
- 2 tablespoon cilantro leaves, chopped

Directions:

1. Into the crockpot, place the hoisin sauce, lemon juice, and shrimps.
2. Season with salt and pepper to taste.
3. Mix to incorporate all ingredients.
4. Close the lid and cook on high for 30 minutes or on low for 2 hours.
5. Garnish with cilantro leaves.

Nutrition Info:

- Calories per serving: 228; Carbohydrates: 6.3g; Protein: 35.8g; Fat: 3.2g; Sugar: 0g; Sodium: 482mg; Fiber: 4.8g

Crab Legs

Servings: 4

Cooking Time: 1 Hour And 30 Minutes

Ingredients:

- 4 pounds king crab legs, broken in half
- 3 lemon wedges
- ¼ cup butter, melted
- ½ cup chicken stock

Directions:

1. In your Crock Pot, mix stock with crab legs and butter, cover and cook on High for 1 hour and 30 minutes.
2. Divide crab legs between bowls, drizzle melted butter all over and serve with lemon wedges on the side.

Nutrition Info:

- calories 100, fat 1, fiber 5, carbs 12, protein 3

Butter Smelt

Servings:4

Cooking Time: 6 Hours

Ingredients:

- 16 oz smelt fillet
- 1/3 cup butter
- 1 teaspoon dried thyme
- 1 teaspoon salt

Directions:

1. Sprinkle the fish with dried thyme and salt and put in the Crock Pot.
2. Add butter and close the lid.
3. Cook the smelt on Low for 6 hours.

Nutrition Info:

- Per Serving: 226 calories, 17.2g protein, 0.2g carbohydrates, 17.4g fat, 0.1g fiber, 191mg cholesterol, 750mg sodium, 7mg potassium

Ginger Cod

Servings: 6

Cooking Time: 5 Hours

Ingredients:

- 6 cod fillets
- 1 teaspoon minced ginger
- 1 tablespoon olive oil
- ¼ teaspoon minced garlic
- ¼ cup chicken stock

Directions:

1. In the mixing bowl mix minced ginger with olive oil and minced garlic.
2. Gently rub the fish fillets with the ginger mixture and put in the Crock Pot.
3. Add chicken stock.
4. Cook the cod on Low for 5 hours.

Nutrition Info:

- Per Serving: 112 calories, 20.1g protein, 0.3g carbohydrates, 3.4g fat, 0g fiber, 55mg cholesterol, 102mg sodium, 5mg potassium

Butter Tilapia

Servings: 4

Cooking Time: 6 Hours

Ingredients:

- 4 tilapia fillets
- ½ cup butter
- 1 teaspoon dried dill
- ½ teaspoon ground black pepper

Directions:

1. Sprinkle the tilapia fillets with dried dill and ground black pepper. Put them in the Crock Pot.
2. Add butter.
3. Cook the tilapia on Low for 6 hours.

Nutrition Info:

- Per Serving: 298 calories, 21.3g protein, 0.3g carbohydrates, 24.1g fat, 0.1g fiber, 116mg cholesterol, 204mg sodium, 18mg potassium

Butter Salmon

Servings: 2

Cooking Time: 1.5 Hours

Ingredients:

- 8 oz salmon fillet
- 3 tablespoons butter
- 1 teaspoon dried sage
- ¼ cup of water

Directions:

1. Churn butter with sage and preheat the mixture until liquid.
2. Then cut the salmon fillets into 2 servings and put in the Crock Pot.
3. Add water and melted butter mixture.
4. Close the lid and cook the salmon on High for 1.5 hours.

Nutrition Info:

- Per Serving: 304 calories, 22.2g protein, 0.2g carbohydrates, 24.3g fat, 0.1g fiber, 96mg cholesterol, 174mg sodium, 444mg potassium.

Pesto Salmon

Servings: 4

Cooking Time: 2.5 Hours

Ingredients:

- 1-pound salmon fillet
- 3 tablespoons pesto sauce
- 1 tablespoon butter
- ¼ cup of water

Directions:

1. Pour water in the Crock Pot.
2. Add butter and 1 tablespoon of pesto.
3. Add salmon and cook the fish on High for 2.5 hours.
4. Chop the cooked salmon and top with remaining pesto sauce.

Nutrition Info:

- Per Serving: 226 calories, 23.2g protein, 0.8g carbohydrates, 14.8g fat, 0.2g fiber, 60mg cholesterol, 142mg sodium, 436mg potassium

Soy Sauce Catfish

Servings: 4

Cooking Time: 5 Hours

Ingredients:

- 1-pound catfish fillet, chopped
- ¼ cup of soy sauce
- 1 jalapeno pepper, diced
- 1 tablespoon olive oil
- 4 tablespoons fish stock

Directions:

1. Sprinkle the catfish with olive oil and put in the Crock Pot.
2. Add soy sauce, jalapeno pepper, and fish stock.
3. Close the lid and cook the meal on Low for 5 hours.

Nutrition Info:

- Per Serving: 195 calories, 19g protein, 1.4g carbohydrates, 12.3g fat, 0.2g fiber, 53mg cholesterol, 981mg sodium, 427mg potassium

Shrimps Boil

Servings: 2

Cooking Time: 45 Minutes

Ingredients:

- ½ cup of water
- 1 tablespoon piri piri sauce
- 1 tablespoon butter
- 7 oz shrimps, peeled

Directions:

1. Pour water in the Crock Pot.
2. Add shrimps and cook them on high for 45 minutes.
3. Then drain water and transfer shrimps in the skillet.
4. Add butter and piri piri sauce.
5. Roast the shrimps for 2-3 minutes on medium heat.

Nutrition Info:

- Per Serving: 174 calories, 22.7g protein, 1.8g carbohydrates, 7.8g fat, 0.1g fiber, 224mg cholesterol, 285mg sodium, 170mg potassium

Spicy Curried Shrimps

Servings:4

Cooking Time: 2 Hours

Ingredients:

- 1 ½ pounds shrimp, shelled and deveined
- 1 tablespoon ghee or butter, melted
- 1 tablespoon curry powder
- 1 teaspoon cayenne pepper
- Salt and pepper to taste

Directions:

1. Place all ingredients in the crockpot.
2. Give a stir to incorporate everything.
3. Close the lid and allow to cook on low for 2 hours or on high for 30 minutes.

Nutrition Info:

- Calories per serving: 207; Carbohydrates:2.2 g; Protein: 35.2g; Fat: 10.5g; Sugar: 0g; Sodium: 325mg; Fiber: 1.6g

Butter Crab

Servings:4

Cooking Time: 4.5 Hours

Ingredients:

- 1-pound crab meat, roughly chopped
- 1 tablespoon fresh parsley, chopped
- 3 tablespoons butter
- 2 tablespoons water

Directions:

1. Melt butter and pour it in the Crock Pot.
2. Add water, parsley, and crab meat.
3. Cook the meal on Low for 4.5 hours.

Nutrition Info:

- Per Serving: 178 calories, 14.3g protein, 2.1g carbohydrates, 10.7g fat, 0g fiber, 84mg cho-lesterol, 771mg sodium, 8mg potassium.

Thyme And Sesame Halibut

Servings:2

Cooking Time: 4 Hours

Ingredients:

- 1 tablespoon lemon juice
- 1 teaspoon thyme
- Salt and pepper to taste
- 8 ounces halibut or mahi-mahi, cut into 2 portions
- 1 tablespoons sesame seeds, toasted

Directions:

1. Line the bottom of the crockpot with a foil.
2. Mix lemon juice, thyme, salt and pepper in a shallow dish.
3. Place the fish and allow to marinate for 2 hours in the fish.
4. Sprinkle the fish with toasted sesame seeds.
5. Arrange the fish in the foil-lined crockpot.
6. Close the lid and cook on high for 2 hours or on low for 4 hours.

Nutrition Info:

- Calories per serving: 238; Carbohydrates: 3.9g; Protein: 23.1g; Fat: 14.9g; Sugar: 0.5g; Sodium:313 mg; Fiber:1.6 g

Crockpot Greek Snapper

Servings: 8

Cooking Time: 4 Hours

Ingredients:

- 3 tablespoons olive oil
- 12 snapper fillets
- 1 tablespoon Greek seasoning
- 24 lemon slices
- Salt and pepper to taste

Directions:

1. Line the bottom of the crockpot with foil.
2. Grease the foil with olive oil
3. Season the snapper fillets with Greek seasoning, salt, and pepper.
4. Arrange lemon slices on top.
5. Close the lid and cook on high for 2 hours and on low for 4 hours.

Nutrition Info:

- Calories per serving: 409; Carbohydrates: 4.3g; Protein:67 g; Fat: 15.3g; Sugar: 0g; Sodium: 246mg; Fiber: 1.8g

Salmon Stew

Servings: 6

Cooking Time: 5 Hours 15 Minutes

Ingredients:

- 2 tablespoons butter
- 2 pounds salmon fillet, cubed
- 2 medium onions, chopped
- Salt and black pepper, to taste
- 2 cups homemade fish broth

Directions:

1. Put all the ingredients in the one pot crock pot and thoroughly mix.
2. Cover and cook on LOW for about 5 hours.

3. Dish out and serve hot.

Nutrition Info:

- Calories: 293 Fat: 8.7g Carbohydrates: 16.3g

Chili Salmon

Servings: 4

Cooking Time: 5 Hours

Ingredients:

- 1-pound salmon fillet, chopped
- 3 oz chili, chopped, canned
- ½ cup of water
- ½ teaspoon salt

Directions:

1. Place all ingredients in the Crock Pot and close the lid.
2. Cook the meal on Low for 5 hours.

Nutrition Info:

- Per Serving: 174 calories, 23.2g protein, 2.5g carbohydrates,8.2g fat, 0.9g fiber, 54mg cholesterol, 453mg sodium, 513mg potassium.

Cinnamon Catfish

Servings: 2

Cooking Time: 2.5 Hours

Ingredients:

- 2 catfish fillets
- 1 teaspoon ground cinnamon
- 1 tablespoon lemon juice
- ½ teaspoon sesame oil
- 1/3 cup water

Directions:

1. Sprinkle the fish fillets with ground cinnamon, lemon juice, and sesame oil.
2. Put the fillets in the Crock Pot in one layer.
3. Add water and close the lid.
4. Cook the meal on High for 2.5 hours.

Nutrition Info:

- Per Serving: 231 calories, 25g protein, 1.1g carbohydrates, 13.3g fat, 0.6g fiber, 75mg cholesterol, 88mg sodium, 528mg potassium.

Creamy Pangasius

Servings: 4

Cooking Time: 2.5 Hours

Ingredients:

- 4 pangasius fillets
- ½ cup cream
- 1 teaspoon cornflour
- 1 tablespoon fish sauce
- 1 teaspoon ground nutmeg

Directions:

1. Coat the fish fillets in the cornflour and sprinkle with ground nutmeg.
2. Put the fish in the Crock Pot.
3. Add cream and fish sauce.
4. Close the lid and cook the meal on High for 2.5

hours.

Nutrition Info:

- Per Serving: 106 calories, 15.5g protein, 1.8g carbohydrates, 4.9g fat, 0.2g fiber, 26mg cholesterol, 617mg sodium, 28mg potassium

Taco Mahi Mahi

Servings: 6

Cooking Time: 6 Hours

Ingredients:

- 2-pounds Mahi Mahi fillets
- 1 tablespoon taco seasonings
- 1 teaspoon fish sauce
- 1/3 cup chicken stock
- 1 tablespoon sunflower oil

Directions:

1. Sprinkle the fish fillets with taco seasonings and fish sauce.
2. Pour sunflower oil in the Crock Pot.
3. Add fish and chicken stock.
4. Close the lid and cook the fish on Low for 6 hours.

Nutrition Info:

- Per Serving: 163 calories, 28.7g protein, 1.4g carbohydrates, 3.8g fat, 0g fiber, 130mg cholesterol, 453mg sodium, 563mg potassium

Garlic Perch

Servings: 4

Cooking Time: 4 Hours

Ingredients:

- 1-pound perch
- 1 teaspoon minced garlic
- 1 tablespoon butter, softened
- 1 tablespoon fish sauce
- ½ cup of water

Directions:

1. In the shallow bowl mix minced garlic, butter, and fish sauce.
2. Rub the perch with a garlic butter mixture and arrange it in the Crock Pot.
3. Add remaining garlic butter mixture and water.
4. Cook the fish on high for 4 hours.

Nutrition Info:

- Per Serving: 161 calories, 28.5g protein, 0.4g carbohydrates, 4.2g fat, 0g fiber, 138mg cholesterol, 458mg sodium, 407mg potassium.

Poached Catfish

Servings: 4

Cooking Time: 3.5 Hours

Ingredients:

- 12 oz catfish fillet
- 1 teaspoon dried rosemary
- 1 cup chicken stock
- 1 teaspoon salt

Directions:

1. Pour the chicken stock in the Crock Pot.
2. Add salt and dried rosemary.
3. Then add catfish fillet and close the lid.
4. Cook the fish on high for 3.5 hours.

Nutrition Info:

- Per Serving: 213 calories, 20.3g protein, 0.8g carbohydrates, 13.9g fat, 0.1g fiber, 69mg cholesterol, 158mg sodium, 392mg potassium

Mustard Cod

Servings: 4

Cooking Time: 3 Hours

Ingredients:

- 4 cod fillets
- 4 teaspoons mustard
- 2 tablespoons sesame oil
- ¼ cup of water

Directions:

1. Mix mustard with sesame oil.
2. Then brush the cod fillets with mustard mixture and transfer in the Crock Pot.
3. Add water and cook the fish on low for 3 hours.

Nutrition Info:

- Per Serving: 166 calories, 20.8g protein, 1.2g carbohydrates, 8.8g fat, 0.5g fiber, 55mg cholesterol, 71mg sodium, 23mg potassium

Garlic Tuna

Servings:4

Cooking Time: 2 Hours

Ingredients:

- 1-pound tuna fillet
- 1 teaspoon garlic powder
- 1 tablespoon olive oil
- ½ cup of water

Directions:

1. Sprinkle the tuna fillet with garlic powder.
2. Then pour olive oil in the skillet and heat it well.
3. Add the tuna and roast it for 1 minute per side.
4. Transfer the tuna in the Crock Pot.
5. Add water and cook it on High for 2 hours.

Nutrition Info:

- Per Serving: 444 calories, 23.9g protein, 0.5g carbohydrates, 38.7g fat, 0.1g fiber, 0mg cholesterol, 1mg sodium, 8mg potassium

Scallops With Sour Cream And Dill

Servings:4

Cooking Time: 2 Hours

Ingredients:

- 1 ¼ pounds scallops
- Salt and pepper to taste
- 3 teaspoons butter
- ¼ cup sour cream
- 1 tablespoon fresh dill

Directions:

1. Add all ingredients into the crockpot.
2. Give a good stir to combine everything.
3. Close the lid and cook on high for 30 minutes or on low for 2 hours.

Nutrition Info:

- Calories per serving: 152; Carbohydrates: 4.3g; Protein: 18.2g; Fat: 5.7g; Sugar: 0.5g; Sodium: 231mg; Fiber: 2.3g

Spicy Basil Shrimp

Servings:4

Cooking Time: 2 Hours

Ingredients:

- 1-pound raw shrimp, shelled and deveined
- Salt and pepper to taste
- 1 tablespoon butter
- ¼ cup packed fresh basil leaves
- ¼ teaspoon cayenne pepper

Directions:

1. Add all ingredients in the crockpot.
2. Give a stir.
3. Close the lid and cook on high for 30 minutes or on low for 2 hours.

Nutrition Info:

- Calories per serving: 144; Carbohydrates: 1.4g; Protein: 23.4g; Fat: 6.2g; Sugar: 0g; Sodium: 126mg; Fiber:0.5 g

Vegetable & Vegetarian Recipes

Garlic Gnocchi 57

Artichoke Dip.................................. 57

Apples Sauté 57

Mushroom Steaks............................ 58

Braised Sesame Spinach 58

Paprika Okra 58

Vegetarian Red Coconut Curry 59

Mashed Turnips............................... 59

Eggplant Parmesan Casserole 59

Sauteed Spinach 60

Creamy Puree................................. 60

Buffalo Cremini Mushrooms 60

Egg Cauliflower 61

Creamy White Mushrooms 61

Garlic Asparagus............................. 61

Asian Broccoli Sauté......................... 62

Curry Couscous................................ 62

Paprika Baby Carrot.......................... 62

Green Peas Puree 63

Cauliflower Curry 63

Baked Onions................................. 63

Spinach With Halloumi Cheese Casserole 64

Sautéed Greens............................... 64

Cauliflower Rice 64

Vegetable & Vegetarian Recipes

Garlic Gnocchi

Servings:4

Cooking Time: 3 Hours

Ingredients:

- 2 cups mozzarella, shredded
- 3 egg yolks, beaten
- 1 teaspoon garlic, minced
- ½ cup heavy cream
- Salt and pepper to taste

Directions:

1. In a mixing bowl, combine the mozzarella and egg yolks.
2. Form gnocchi balls and place in the fridge to set.
3. Boil a pot of water over high flame and drop the gnocchi balls for 30 seconds. Take them out and transfer to the crockpot.
4. Into the crockpot add the garlic and heavy cream.
5. Season with salt and pepper to taste.
6. Close the lid and cook on low for 3 hours or on high for 1 hour.

Nutrition Info:

- Calories per serving: 178; Carbohydrates: 4.1g; Protein:20.5 g; Fat: 8.9g; Sugar:0.3g; Sodium: 421mg; Fiber: 2.1g

Artichoke Dip

Servings:6

Cooking Time: 6 Hours

Ingredients:

- 2 cups Cheddar cheese, shredded
- 1 cup of coconut milk
- 1-pound artichoke, drained, chopped
- 1 tablespoon Ranch dressing

Directions:

1. Put all ingredients in the Crock Pot.
2. Mix them gently and close the lid.
3. Cook the artichoke dip on Low for 6 hours.

Nutrition Info:

- Per Serving: 280 calories, 12.8g protein, 10.8g carbohydrates, 22.1g fat, 5g fiber, 40mg cholesterol, 325mg sodium, 422mg potassium.

Apples Sauté

Servings:4

Cooking Time: 2 Hours

Ingredients:

- 4 cups apples, chopped
- 1 cup of water
- 1 teaspoon ground cinnamon
- 1 teaspoon sugar

Directions:

1. Put all ingredients in the Crock Pot.
2. Cook the apple sauté for 2 hours on High.
3. When the meal is cooked, let it cool until warm.

Nutrition Info:

- Per Serving: 121 calories, 0.6g protein, 32.3g carbohydrates, 0.4g fat, 5.7g fiber, 0mg cholesterol, 4mg sodium, 242mg potassium.

Mushroom Steaks

Servings:4

Cooking Time: 2 Hours

Ingredients:

- 4 Portobello mushrooms
- 1 tablespoon avocado oil
- 1 tablespoon lemon juice
- 2 tablespoons coconut cream
- ½ teaspoon ground black pepper

Directions:

1. Slice Portobello mushrooms into steaks and sprinkle with avocado oil, lemon juice, coconut cream, and ground black pepper.
2. Then arrange the mushroom steaks in the Crock Pot in one layer (you will need to cook all mushroom steaks by 2 times).
3. Cook the meal on High for 1 hour.

Nutrition Info:

- Per Serving: 43 calories, 3.3g protein, 3.9g carbohydrates, 2.3g fat, 1.4g fiber, 0mg cholesterol, 2mg sodium, 339mg potassium.

Braised Sesame Spinach

Servings:4

Cooking Time: 35 Minutes

Ingredients:

- 1 tablespoon sesame seeds
- ¼ cup of soy sauce
- 2 tablespoons sesame oil
- 4 cups spinach, chopped
- 1 cup of water

Directions:

1. Pour water in the Crock Pot.
2. Add spinach and cook it on High for 35 minutes.
3. After this, drain water and transfer the spinach in the big bowl.
4. Add soy sauce, sesame oil, and sesame seeds.
5. Carefully mix the spinach and transfer in the serving plates/bowls.

Nutrition Info:

- Per Serving: 88 calories, 2.3g protein, 2.8g carbohydrates, 8.1g fat, 1.1g fiber, 2.8mg cholesterol, 924mg sodium, 213mg potassium.

Paprika Okra

Servings:4

Cooking Time: 40 Minutes

Ingredients:

- 4 cups okra, sliced
- 1 tablespoon smoked paprika
- 1 teaspoon salt
- 2 tablespoons coconut oil
- 1 cup organic almond milk

Directions:

1. Pour almond milk in the Crock Pot.
2. Add coconut oil, salt, and smoked paprika.
3. Then add sliced okra and gently mix the ingredients.
4. Cook the okra on High for 40 minutes. Then cooked okra should be tender but not soft.

Nutrition Info:

- Per Serving: 119 calories, 2.4g protein, 10.4g carbohydrates, 7.8g fat, 3.9g fiber, 0mg cholesterol, 624mg sodium, 340mg potassium.

Vegetarian Red Coconut Curry

Servings:4

Cooking Time: 3 Hours

Ingredients:

- 1 cup broccoli florets
- 1 large handful spinach, rinsed
- 1 tablespoon red curry paste
- 1 cup coconut cream
- 1 teaspoon garlic, minced

Directions:

1. Combine all ingredients in the crockpot.
2. Close the lid and cook on low for 3 hours or on high for 1 hour.

Nutrition Info:

- Calories per serving: 226; Carbohydrates: 8g; Protein: 5.2g; Fat:21.4 g; Sugar: 0.4g; Sodium: 341mg; Fiber:4.3 g

Mashed Turnips

Servings:6

Cooking Time: 7 Hours

Ingredients:

- 3-pounds turnip, chopped
- 3 cups of water
- 1 tablespoon vegan butter
- 1 tablespoon chives, chopped
- 2 oz Parmesan, grated

Directions:

1. Put turnips in the Crock Pot.
2. Add water and cook the vegetables on low for 7 hours.
3. Then drain water and mash the turnips.
4. Add chives, butter, and Parmesan.
5. Carefully stir the mixture until butter and Parmesan are melted.

6. Then add chives. Mix the mashed turnips again.

Nutrition Info:

- Per Serving: 162 calories, 8.6g protein, 15.1g carbohydrates, 8.1g fat, 4.1g fiber, 22mg cholesterol, 475mg sodium, 490mg potassium.

Eggplant Parmesan Casserole

Servings:3

Cooking Time: 3 Hours

Ingredients:

- 1 medium eggplant, sliced
- 1 large egg
- Salt and pepper to taste
- 1 cup almond flour
- 1 cup parmesan cheese

Directions:

1. Place the eggplant slices in the crockpot.
2. Pour in the eggs and season with salt and pepper.
3. Stir in the almond flour and sprinkle with parmesan cheese.
4. Stir to combine everything.
5. Close the lid and cook on low for 3 hours or on high for 2 hours.

Nutrition Info:

- Calories per serving: 212; Carbohydrates: 17g; Protein: 15g; Fat:12.1 g; Sugar: 1.2g; Sodium: 231mg; Fiber:8.1 g

Sauteed Spinach

Servings: 3

Cooking Time: 1 Hour

Ingredients:

- 3 cups spinach
- 1 tablespoon vegan butter, softened
- 2 cups of water
- 2 oz Parmesan, grated
- 1 teaspoon pine nuts, crushed

Directions:

1. Chop the spinach and put it in the Crock Pot.
2. Add water and close the lid.
3. Cook the spinach on High for 1 hour.
4. Then drain water and put the cooked spinach in the bowl.
5. Add pine nuts, Parmesan, and butter.
6. Carefully mix the spinach.

Nutrition Info:

- Per Serving: 108 calories, 7.1g protein, 1.9g carbohydrates, 8.7g fat, 0.7g fiber, 24mg cholesterol, 231mg sodium, 176mg potassium.

Creamy Puree

Servings: 4

Cooking Time: 4 Hours

Ingredients:

- 2 cups potatoes, chopped
- 3 cups of water
- 1 tablespoon vegan butter
- ¼ cup cream
- 1 teaspoon salt

Directions:

1. Pour water in the Crock Pot.
2. Add potatoes and salt.
3. Cook the vegetables on high for 4 hours.
4. Then drain water, add butter, and cream.
5. Mash the potatoes until smooth.

Nutrition Info:

- Per Serving: 87 calories, 1.4g protein, 12.3g carbohydrates, 3.8g fat, 1.8g fiber, 10mg cholesterol, 617mg sodium, 314mg potassium

Buffalo Cremini Mushrooms

Servings: 4

Cooking Time: 6 Hours

Ingredients:

- 3 cups cremini mushrooms, trimmed
- 2 oz buffalo sauce
- ½ cup of water
- 2 tablespoons coconut oil

Directions:

1. Pour water in the Crock Pot.
2. Melt the coconut oil in the skillet.
3. Add mushrooms and roast them for 3-4 minutes per side. Transfer the roasted mushrooms in the Crock Pot.
4. Cook them on Low for 4 hours.
5. Then add buffalo sauce and carefully mix.
6. Cook the mushrooms for 2 hours on low.

Nutrition Info:

- Per Serving: 79 calories, 1.4g protein, 3.2g carbohydrates, 6.9g fat, 0.8g fiber, 0mg cholesterol, 458mg sodium, 242mg potassium.

Egg Cauliflower

Servings:2

Cooking Time: 4 Hours

Ingredients:

- 2 cups cauliflower, shredded
- 4 eggs, beaten
- 1 tablespoon vegan butter
- ½ teaspoon salt

Directions:

1. Mix eggs with salt.
2. Put the shredded cauliflower in the Crock Pot.
3. Add eggs and vegan butter. Gently mix the mixture.
4. Close the lid and cook the meal on low for 4 hours. Stir the cauliflower with the help of the fork every 1 hour.

Nutrition Info:

- Per Serving: 176 calories, 13.5g protein, 9.9g carbohydrates, 9.7g fat, 2.6g fiber, 372mg cholesterol, 746mg sodium, 421mg potassium.

Creamy White Mushrooms

Servings:4

Cooking Time: 8 Hours

Ingredients:

- 1-pound white mushrooms, chopped
- 1 cup cream
- 1 teaspoon chili flakes
- 1 teaspoon ground black pepper
- 1 tablespoon dried parsley

Directions:

1. Put all ingredients in the Crock Pot.
2. Cook the mushrooms on low for 8 hours.
3. When the mushrooms are cooked, transfer them in the serving bowls and cool for 10-15 minutes.

Nutrition Info:

- Per Serving: 65 calories, 4.1g protein, 6g carbohydrates, 3.7g fat, 1.3g fiber, 11mg cholesterol, 27mg sodium, 396mg potassium.

Garlic Asparagus

Servings:5

Cooking Time: 6 Hours

Ingredients:

- 1-pound asparagus, trimmed
- 1 teaspoon salt
- 1 teaspoon garlic powder
- 1 tablespoon vegan butter
- 1 ½ cup vegetable stock

Directions:

1. Chop the asparagus roughly and sprinkle with salt and garlic powder.
2. Put the vegetables in the Crock Pot.
3. Add vegan butter and vegetable stock. Close the lid.
4. Cook the asparagus on Low for 6 hours.

Nutrition Info:

- Per Serving: 33 calories, 2.3g protein, 6.1g carbohydrates, 1g fat, 2g fiber, 0mg cholesterol, 687mg sodium, 190mg potassium.

Asian Broccoli Sauté

Servings:4

Cooking Time: 3 Hours

Ingredients:

- 1 tablespoon coconut oil
- 1 head broccoli, cut into florets
- 1 tablespoon coconut aminos or soy sauce
- 1 teaspoon ginger, grated
- Salt and pepper to taste

Directions:

1. Place the ingredients in the crockpot.
2. Toss everything to combine.
3. Close the lid and cook on low for 3 hours or on high for an hour.
4. Once cooked, sprinkle with sesame seeds or sesame oil.

Nutrition Info:

- Calories per serving: 62; Carbohydrates:3.6 g; Protein: 1.8g; Fat: 4.3g; Sugar:0.3 g; Sodium: 87mg; Fiber: 2.1g

Curry Couscous

Servings:4

Cooking Time: 20 Minutes

Ingredients:

- 1 cup of water
- 1 cup couscous
- ½ cup coconut cream
- 1 teaspoon salt

Directions:

1. Put all ingredients in the Crock Pot and close the lid.
2. Cook the couscous on High for 20 minutes.

Nutrition Info:

- Per Serving: 182 calories, 5.8g protein, 34.4g carbohydrates, 2g fat, 2.2g fiber, 6mg cholesterol, 597mg sodium, 84mg potassium.

Paprika Baby Carrot

Servings:2

Cooking Time: 2.5 Hours

Ingredients:

- 1 tablespoon ground paprika
- 2 cups baby carrot
- 1 teaspoon cumin seeds
- 1 cup of water
- 1 teaspoon vegan butter

Directions:

1. Pour water in the Crock Pot.
2. Add baby carrot, cumin seeds, and ground paprika.
3. Close the lid and cook the carrot on High for 2.5 hours.
4. Then drain water, add butter, and shake the vegetables.

Nutrition Info:

- Per Serving: 60 calories, 1.6g protein, 8.6g carbohydrates, 2.7g fat, 4.2g fiber, 5mg cholesterol, 64mg sodium, 220mg potassium.

Green Peas Puree

Servings:2

Cooking Time: 1 Hour

Ingredients:

- 2 cups green peas, frozen
- 1 tablespoon coconut oil
- 1 teaspoon smoked paprika
- 1 cup vegetable stock

Directions:

1. Put green peas, smoked paprika, and vegetable stock in the Crock Pot.
2. Cook the ingredients in high for 1 hour.
3. Then drain the liquid and mash the green peas with the help of the potato masher.
4. Add coconut oil and carefully stir the cooked puree.

Nutrition Info:

- Per Serving: 184 calories, 8.4g protein, 21.9g carbohydrates, 7.8g fat, 7.8g fiber, 0mg cholesterol, 389mg sodium, 386mg potassium.

Cauliflower Curry

Servings:4

Cooking Time: 2 Hours

Ingredients:

- 4 cups cauliflower
- 1 tablespoon curry paste
- 2 cups of coconut milk

Directions:

1. In the mixing bowl mix coconut milk with curry paste until smooth.
2. Put cauliflower in the Crock Pot.
3. Pour the curry liquid over the cauliflower and close the lid.
4. Cook the meal on High for 2 hours.

Nutrition Info:

- Per Serving: 236 calories, 4.9g protein, 13g carbohydrates, 30.9g fat, 5.1g fiber, 0mg cholesterol, 48mg sodium, 619mg potassium.

Baked Onions

Servings:4

Cooking Time: 2 Hours

Ingredients:

- 4 onions, peeled
- 1 tablespoon coconut oil
- 1 teaspoon salt
- 1 teaspoon brown sugar
- 1 cup coconut cream

Directions:

1. Put coconut oil in the Crock Pot.
2. Then make the small cuts in the onions with the help of the knife and put in the Crock Pot in one layer.
3. Sprinkle the vegetables with salt, and brown sugar.
4. Add coconut cream and close the lid.
5. Cook the onions on High for 2 hours.

Nutrition Info:

- Per Serving: 214 calories, 2.6g protein, 14.3g carbohydrates, 17.8g fat, 3.7g fiber, 0mg cholesterol, 595mg sodium, 320mg potassium.

Spinach With Halloumi Cheese Casserole

Servings:4

Cooking Time: 2 Hours

Ingredients:

- 1 package spinach, rinsed
- ½ cup walnuts, chopped
- Salt and pepper to taste
- 1 tablespoon balsamic vinegar
- 1 ½ cups halloumi cheese, grated

Directions:

1. Place spinach and walnuts in the crockpot.
2. Season with salt and pepper. Drizzle with balsamic vinegar.
3. Top with halloumi cheese and cook on low for 2 hours or on high for 30 minutes

Nutrition Info:

- Calories per serving: 560; Carbohydrates: 7g; Protein:21 g; Fat: 47g; Sugar:2.1 g; Sodium: 231mg; Fiber:3 g

Sautéed Greens

Servings:4

Cooking Time: 1 Hour

Ingredients:

- 1 cup spinach, chopped
- 2 cups collard greens, chopped
- 1 cup Swiss chard, chopped
- 2 cups of water
- ½ cup half and half

Directions:

1. Put spinach, collard greens, and Swiss chard in the Crock Pot.
2. Add water and close the lid.
3. Cook the greens on High for 1 hour.

4. Then drain water and transfer the greens in the bowl.
5. Bring the half and half to boil and pour over greens.
6. Carefully mix the greens.

Nutrition Info:

- Per Serving: 49 calories, 1.8g protein, 3.2g carbohydrates, 3.7g fat, 1.1g fiber, 11mg cholesterol, 45mg sodium, 117mg potassium.

Cauliflower Rice

Servings:6

Cooking Time: 2 Hours

Ingredients:

- 4 cups cauliflower, shredded
- 1 cup vegetable stock
- 1 cup of water
- 1 tablespoon cream cheese
- 1 teaspoon dried oregano

Directions:

1. Put all ingredients in the Crock Pot.
2. Close the lid and cook the cauliflower rice on High for 2 hours.

Nutrition Info:

- Per Serving: 25 calories, 0.8g protein, 3.9g carbohydrates, 0.8g fat, 1.8g fiber, 2mg cholesterol, 153mg sodium, 211mg potassium

Snack Recipes

Bean Dip 66

Cinnamon Pecans Snack 66

Caramel Milk Dip 66

Onion Dip(3) 67

White Bean Spread 67

Roasted Parmesan Green Beans 67

Lemony Artichokes 68

Almond Buns 68

Spaghetti Squash 68

Salsa Beans Dip 69

Beans Spread 69

Crispy Sweet Potatoes With Paprika 69

Salmon Bites 70

Almond Bowls 70

Spicy Dip 70

Apple Dip 70

Beer And Cheese Dip 71

Almond Spread 71

Slow-cooked Lemon Peel 71

Apple Sausage Snack 71

Spinach Dip(2) 72

Cheese Onion Dip 72

Spinach And Walnuts Dip 72

Apple Jelly Sausage Snack 73

Bourbon Sausage Bites 73

Snack Recipes

Bean Dip

Servings: 56

Cooking Time: 3 Hours

Ingredients:

- 16 ounces Mexican cheese
- 5 ounces canned green chilies
- 16 ounces canned refried beans
- 2 pounds tortilla chips
- Cooking spray

Directions:

1. Grease your Crock Pot with cooking spray, line it, add Mexican cheese, green chilies and refried beans, stir, cover and cook on Low for 3 hours.
2. Divide into bowls and serve with tortilla chips on the side.

Nutrition Info:

- calories 120, fat 2, fiber 1, carbs 14, protein 3

Cinnamon Pecans Snack

Servings: 2

Cooking Time: 3 Hours

Ingredients:

- ½ tablespoon cinnamon powder
- ¼ cup water
- ½ tablespoon avocado oil
- ½ teaspoon chili powder
- 2 cups pecans

Directions:

1. In your Crock Pot, mix the pecans with the cinnamon and the other ingredients, toss, put the lid on and cook on Low for 3 hours.
2. Divide the pecans into bowls and serve as a snack.

Nutrition Info:

- calories 172, fat 3, fiber 5, carbs 8, protein 2

Caramel Milk Dip

Servings: 4

Cooking Time: 2 Hours

Ingredients:

- 1 cup butter
- 12 oz. condensed milk
- 2 cups brown sugar
- 1 cup of corn syrup

Directions:

1. Add butter, milk, corn syrup, and sugar to the Crock Pot.
2. Put the cooker's lid on and set the cooking time to 2 hours on High settings.
3. Serve warm.

Nutrition Info:

- Per Serving: Calories: 172, Total Fat: 2g, Fiber: 6g, Total Carbs: 12g, Protein: 4g

Onion Dip(3)

Servings: 2

Cooking Time: 8 Hours

Ingredients:

- 2 cups yellow onions, chopped
- A pinch of salt and black pepper
- 1 tablespoon olive oil
- ½ cup heavy cream
- 2 tablespoons mayonnaise

Directions:

1. In your Crock Pot, mix the onions with the cream and the other ingredients, whisk, put the lid on and cook on Low for 8 hours.
2. Divide into bowls and serve as a party dip.

Nutrition Info:

- calories 240, fat 4, fiber 4, carbs 9, protein 7

White Bean Spread

Servings: 4

Cooking Time: 7 Hours

Ingredients:

- ½ cup white beans, dried
- 2 tablespoons cashews, chopped
- 1 teaspoon apple cider vinegar
- 1 cup veggie stock
- 1 tablespoon water

Directions:

1. In your Crock Pot, mix beans with cashews and stock, stir, cover and cook on Low for 6 hours.
2. Drain, transfer to your food processor, add vinegar and water, pulse well, divide into bowls and serve as a spread.

Nutrition Info:

- calories 221, fat 6, fiber 5, carbs 19, protein 3

Roasted Parmesan Green Beans

Servings: 8 (4.4 Ounces Per Serving)

Cooking Time: 4 Hours And 5 Minutes

Ingredients:

- 2 lbs. green beans, fresh, trimmed
- 2 tablespoons olive oil
- 1 teaspoon salt and black pepper
- ½ cup Parmesan cheese, grated

Directions:

1. Rinse and pat dry green beans with paper towel. Drizzle with olive oil and sprinkle with salt and pepper. Using your fingers coat the beans evenly with olive oil and spread them out do not overlap them. Place green beans in greased Crock-Pot. Sprinkle with Parmesan cheese. Cover and cook on HIGH for 3-4 hours. Serve.

Nutrition Info:

- Calories: 91.93, Total Fat: 5.41 g, Saturated Fat: 1.6 g, Cholesterol: 5.5 mg, Sodium: 337.43 mg, Potassium: 247.12 mg, Total Carbohydrates: 6.16 g, Fiber: 3.06 g, Sugar: 3.75 g, Protein: 4.48 g

Lemony Artichokes

Servings: 4 (5.2 Ounces Per Serving)

Cooking Time: 4 Hours And 10 Minutes

Ingredients:

- 4 artichokes
- 2 tablespoons coconut butter, melted
- 3 tablespoons lemon juice
- 1 teaspoon sea salt
- Ground black pepper to taste

Directions:

1. Wash the artichokes. Pull off the outermost leaves until you get to the lighter yellow leaves. Cut off the top third or so of the artichokes. Trim the bottom of the stems. Place in Crock-Pot. Mix together lemon juice, salt, and melted coconut butter and pour over artichokes. Cover and cook on LOW for 6-8 hours or on HIGH for 3-4 hours. Serve.

Nutrition Info:

- Calories: 113.58, Total Fat: 5.98 g, Saturated Fat: 3.7 g, Cholesterol: 15.27 mg, Sodium: 702.59 mg, Potassium: 487.2 mg, Total Carbohydrates: 8.25 g, Fiber: 6.95 g, Sugar: 1.56 g, Protein: 4.29 g

Almond Buns

Servings: 6 (1.9 Ounces Per Serving)

Cooking Time: 20 Minutes

Ingredients:

- 3 cups almond flour
- 5 tablespoons butter
- 1 ½ teaspoons sweetener of your choice (optional)
- 2 eggs
- 1 ½ teaspoons baking powder

Directions:

1. In a mixing bowl, combine the dry ingredients. In another bowl, whisk the eggs. Add melted butter to mixture and mix well. Divide almond mixture equally into 6 parts. Grease the bottom of Crock-Pot and place in 6 almond buns. Cover and cook on HIGH for 2 to 2 ½ hours or LOW for 4 to 4 ½ hours. Serve hot.

Nutrition Info:

- Calories: 219.35, Total Fat: 20.7 g, Saturated Fat: 7.32 g, Cholesterol: 87.44 mg, Sodium: 150.31 mg, Potassium: 145.55 mg, Total Carbohydrates: 4.59 g, Fiber: 1.8 g, Sugar: 1.6 g, Protein: 6.09 g

Spaghetti Squash

Servings: 6 (6.8 Ounces)

Cooking Time: 6 Hours

Ingredients:

- 1 spaghetti squash (vegetable spaghetti)
- 4 tablespoon olive oil
- 1 ¾ cups water
- Sea salt

Directions:

1. Slice the squash in half lengthwise and scoop out the seeds. Drizzle the halves with olive oil and season with sea salt. Place the squash in Crock-Pot and add the water. Close the lid and cook on LOW for 4-6 hours. Remove the squash and allow it to cool for about 30 minutes. Use a fork to scrape out spaghetti squash.

Nutrition Info:

- Calories: 130.59, Total Fat: 9.11 g, Saturated Fat: 1.27 g, Cholesterol: 0 mg, Sodium: 6.79 mg, Potassium: 399.95 mg, Total Carbohydrates: 13.26 g, Fiber: 2.27 g, Sugar: 2.49 g, Protein: 1.13 g

Salsa Beans Dip

Servings: 2

Cooking Time: 1 Hour

Ingredients:

- ¼ cup salsa
- 1 cup canned red kidney beans, drained and rinsed
- ½ cup mozzarella, shredded
- 1 tablespoon green onions, chopped

Directions:

1. In your Crock Pot, mix the salsa with the beans and the other ingredients, toss, put the lid on cook on High for 1 hour.
2. Divide into bowls and serve as a party dip

Nutrition Info:

- calories 302, fat 5, fiber 10, carbs 16, protein 6

Beans Spread

Servings: 2

Cooking Time: 6 Hours

Ingredients:

- 1 cup canned black beans, drained
- 2 tablespoons tahini paste
- ½ teaspoon balsamic vinegar
- ¼ cup veggie stock
- ½ tablespoon olive oil

Directions:

1. In your Crock Pot, mix the beans with the tahini paste and the other ingredients, toss, put the lid on and cook on Low for 6 hours.
2. Transfer to your food processor, blend well, divide into bowls and serve.

Nutrition Info:

- calories 221, fat 6, fiber 5, carbs 19, protein 3

Crispy Sweet Potatoes With Paprika

Servings: 4 (3.2 Ounces Per Serving)

Cooking Time: 4 Hours And 45 Minutes

Ingredients:

- 2 medium sweet potatoes
- 2 tablespoons olive oil
- 1 teaspoon Cayenne pepper, optional
- 1 tablespoon nutritional yeast, optional
- Sea salt

Directions:

1. Wash and peel the sweet potatoes. Slice them into wedges. In a bowl, mix the potatoes with the other ingredients. Grease the bottom of Crock-Pot and place the sweet potato wedges in it. Cover and cook on LOW for 4- 4 ½ hours. Serve hot.

Nutrition Info:

- Calories: 120.72, Total Fat: 7.02 g, Saturated Fat: 0.98 g, Cholesterol: 0 mg, Sodium: 37.07 mg, Potassium: 260.14 mg, Total Carbohydrates: 9.06 g, Fiber: 2.57 g, Sugar: 2.9 g

Salmon Bites

Servings: 2

Cooking Time: 2 Hours

Ingredients:

- 1 pound salmon fillets, boneless
- ¼ cup chili sauce
- A pinch of salt and black pepper
- ½ teaspoon turmeric powder
- 2 tablespoons grape jelly

Directions:

1. In your Crock Pot, mix the salmon with the chili sauce and the other ingredients, toss gently, put the lid on and cook on High for 2 hours.
2. Serve as an appetizer.

Nutrition Info:

- calories 200, fat 6, fiber 3, carbs 15, protein 12

Almond Bowls

Servings: 2

Cooking Time: 4 Hours

Ingredients:

- 1 tablespoon cinnamon powder
- 1 cup sugar
- 2 cups almonds
- ½ cup water
- ½ teaspoons vanilla extract

Directions:

1. In your Crock Pot, mix the almonds with the cinnamon and the other ingredients, toss, put the lid on and cook on Low for 4 hours.
2. Divide into bowls and serve as a snack.

Nutrition Info:

- calories 260, fat 3, fiber 4, carbs 12, protein 8

Spicy Dip

Servings: 10

Cooking Time: 3 Hours

Ingredients:

- 1 pound spicy sausage, chopped
- 8 ounces cream cheese, soft
- 8 ounces sour cream
- 20 ounces canned tomatoes and green chilies, chopped

Directions:

1. In your Crock Pot, mix sausage with cream cheese, sour cream and tomatoes and chilies, stir, cover and cook on Low for 3 hours.
2. Divide into bowls and serve as a snack.

Nutrition Info:

- calories 300, fat 12, fiber 7, carbs 30, protein 34

Apple Dip

Servings: 8

Cooking Time: 1 Hour And 30 Minutes

Ingredients:

- 5 apples, peeled and chopped
- ½ teaspoon cinnamon powder
- 12 ounces jarred caramel sauce
- A pinch of nutmeg, ground

Directions:

1. In your Crock Pot, mix apples with cinnamon, caramel sauce and nutmeg, stir, cover and cook on High for 1 hour and 30 minutes.
2. Divide into bowls and serve.

Nutrition Info:

- calories 200, fat 3, fiber 6, carbs 10, protein 5

Beer And Cheese Dip

Servings: 10

Cooking Time: 1 Hour

Ingredients:

- 12 ounces cream cheese
- 6 ounces beer
- 4 cups cheddar cheese, shredded
- 1 tablespoon chives, chopped

Directions:

1. In your Crock Pot, mix cream cheese with beer and cheddar, stir, cover and cook on Low for 1 hour.
2. Stir your dip, add chives, divide into bowls and serve.

Nutrition Info:

- calories 212, fat 4, fiber 7, carbs 16, protein 5

Almond Spread

Servings: 2

Cooking Time: 8 Hours

Ingredients:

- ¼ cup almonds
- 1 cup heavy cream
- ½ teaspoon nutritional yeast flakes
- A pinch of salt and black pepper

Directions:

1. In your Crock Pot, mix the almonds with the cream and the other ingredients, toss, put the lid on and cook on Low for 8 hours.
2. Transfer to a blender, pulse well, divide into bowls and serve.

Nutrition Info:

- calories 270, fat 4, fiber 4, carbs 8, protein 10

Slow-cooked Lemon Peel

Servings: 80 Pieces

Cooking Time: 4 Hrs

Ingredients:

- 5 big lemons, peel cut into strips
- 2 and ¼ cups white sugar
- 5 cups of water

Directions:

1. Spread the lemon peel in the Crock Pot and top it with sugar and water.
2. Put the cooker's lid on and set the cooking time to 4 hours on Low settings.
3. Drain the cooked peel and serve.

Nutrition Info:

- Per Serving: Calories: 7, Total Fat: 1g, Fiber: 1g, Total Carbs: 2g, Protein: 1g

Apple Sausage Snack

Servings: 15

Cooking Time: 2 Hrs

Ingredients:

- 2 lbs. sausages, sliced
- 18 oz. apple jelly
- 9 oz. Dijon mustard

Directions:

1. Add sausage slices, apple jelly, and mustard to the Crock Pot.
2. Put the cooker's lid on and set the cooking time to 2 hours on Low settings.
3. Serve fresh.

Nutrition Info:

- Per Serving: Calories: 200, Total Fat: 3g, Fiber: 1g, Total Carbs: 9g, Protein: 10g

Spinach Dip(2)

Servings: 2

Cooking Time: 1 Hour

Ingredients:

- 2 tablespoons heavy cream
- ½ cup Greek yogurt
- ½ pound baby spinach
- 2 garlic cloves, minced
- Salt and black pepper to the taste

Directions:

1. In your Crock Pot, mix the spinach with the cream and the other ingredients, toss, put the lid on and cook on High for 1 hour.
2. Blend using an immersion blender, divide into bowls and serve as a party dip.

Nutrition Info:

- calories 221, fat 5, fiber 7, carbs 12, protein 5

Cheese Onion Dip

Servings: 6

Cooking Time: 1 Hour

Ingredients:

- 8 oz. cream cheese, soft
- ¾ cup sour cream
- 1 cup cheddar cheese, shredded
- 10 bacon slices, cooked and chopped
- 2 yellow onions, chopped

Directions:

1. Add cream cheese, bacon and all other ingredients to the Crock Pot.
2. Put the cooker's lid on and set the cooking time to 1 hour on High settings.
3. Serve.

Nutrition Info:

- Per Serving: Calories: 222, Total Fat: 4g, Fiber: 6g, Total Carbs: 17g, Protein: 4g

Spinach And Walnuts Dip

Servings: 2

Cooking Time: 2 Hours

Ingredients:

- ½ cup heavy cream
- ½ cup walnuts, chopped
- 1 cup baby spinach
- 1 garlic clove, chopped
- 1 tablespoon mayonnaise
- Salt and black pepper to the taste

Directions:

1. In your Crock Pot, mix the spinach with the walnuts and the other ingredients, toss, put the lid on and cook on High for 2 hours.
2. Blend using an immersion blender, divide into bowls and serve as a party dip.

Nutrition Info:

- calories 260, fat 4, fiber 2, carbs 12, protein 5

Apple Jelly Sausage Snack

Servings: 15

Cooking Time: 2 Hours

Ingredients:

- 2 pounds sausages, sliced
- 18 ounces apple jelly
- 9 ounces Dijon mustard

Directions:

1. Place sausage slices in your Crock Pot, add apple jelly and mustard, toss to coat well, cover and cook on Low for 2 hours.
2. Divide into bowls and serve as a snack.

Nutrition Info:

- calories 200, fat 3, fiber 1, carbs 9, protein 10

Bourbon Sausage Bites

Servings: 12

Cooking Time: 3 Hours And 5 Minutes

Ingredients:

- 1/3 cup bourbon
- 1 pound smoked sausage, sliced
- 12 ounces chili sauce
- ¼ cup brown sugar
- 2 tablespoons yellow onion, grated

Directions:

1. Heat up a pan over medium-high heat, add sausage slices, brown them for 2 minutes on each side, drain them on paper towels and transfer to your Crock Pot.
2. Add chili sauce, sugar, onion and bourbon, toss to coat, cover and cook on Low for 3 hours.
3. Divide into bowls and serve as a snack.

Nutrition Info:

- calories 190, fat 11, fiber 1, carbs 12, protein 5

Dessert Recipes

Orange Bowls.................................75

Clove Pastry Wheels.........................75

Cinnamon Plum Jam...........................75

Avocado Jelly................................76

Marshmallow Hot Drink........................76

Cardamom Apple Jam...........................76

Melon Pudding...............................77

Amaretto Pear Butter........................77

Dates And Rice Pudding......................77

Cardamom Apples.............................77

Apple Granola Crumble.......................78

Chocolate Pudding...........................78

Blueberries Jam.............................78

Tarragon Peach Confiture....................78

Lentil Pudding..............................79

Pear Apple Jam..............................79

Bounty......................................79

Ricotta Bake With Dates And Nuts............80

Braised Pears...............................80

Cocoa Peanut Candies........................80

Banana Muffins..............................81

Caramel Sauce Poached Pears.................81

Baked Camembert.............................81

Blueberry Tapioca Pudding...................82

Fluffy Vegan Cream..........................82

Dessert Recipes

Orange Bowls

Servings: 2

Cooking Time: 3 Hours

Ingredients:

- ½ pound oranges, peeled and cut into segments
- 1 cup heavy cream
- ½ tablespoon almonds, chopped
- 1 tablespoon chia seeds
- 1 tablespoon sugar

Directions:

1. In your Crock Pot, mix the oranges with the cream and the other ingredients, toss, put the lid on and cook on Low for 3 hours.
2. Divide into bowls and serve.

Nutrition Info:

- calories 170, fat 0, fiber 2, carbs 7, protein 4

Clove Pastry Wheels

Servings:4

Cooking Time: 3 Hours

Ingredients:

- 1 teaspoon ground clove
- 4 oz puff pastry
- 1 tablespoon brown sugar
- 1 tablespoon butter, softened

Directions:

1. Roll up the puff pastry into a square.
2. Then grease the puff pastry with butter and sprinkle with ground clove.
3. Roll it in the shape of a log and cut it into pieces (wheels).
4. Put the baking paper at the bottom of the Crock Pot.
5. Then put puff pastry wheels inside in one layer and close the lid.
6. Cook the meal on High for 3 hours.

Nutrition Info:

- Per Serving: 192 calories, 2.1g protein, 15.3g carbohydrates, 13.8g fat, 0.6g fiber, 8mg cholesterol, 93mg sodium, 27mg potassium.

Cinnamon Plum Jam

Servings:6

Cooking Time: 6 Hours

Ingredients:

- 4 cups plums, pitted, halved
- 1 tablespoon ground cinnamon
- ½ cup brown sugar
- 1 teaspoon vanilla extract

Directions:

1. Put all ingredients in the Crock Pot and gently mix.
2. Close the lid and cook it on Low for 6 hours.

Nutrition Info:

- Per Serving: 71 calories, 0.4g protein, 18.2g carbohydrates, 0.1g fat, 1.2g fiber, 0mg cholesterol, 4mg sodium, 91mg potassium.

Avocado Jelly

Servings:2

Cooking Time: 1.5 Hours

Ingredients:

- 1 avocado, pitted, chopped
- 1 cup of orange juice
- 1 tablespoon gelatin
- 3 tablespoons brown sugar

Directions:

1. Pour orange juice in the Crock Pot.
2. Add brown sugar and cook the liquid on High for 1.5 hours.
3. Then add gelatin and stir the mixture until smooth.
4. After this, blend the avocado until smooth, add orange juice liquid and mix until homogenous.
5. Pour it in the cups and refrigerate until solid.

Nutrition Info:

- Per Serving: 324 calories, 5.8g protein, 34.8g carbohydrates, 19.9g fat, 7g fiber, 0mg cholesterol, 18mg sodium, 754mg potassium.

Marshmallow Hot Drink

Servings:3

Cooking Time: 5 Hours

Ingredients:

- ½ cup of chocolate chips
- 4 oz marshmallows
- 1 teaspoon butter
- 2 cups of milk

Directions:

1. Put all ingredients in the Crock Pot and close the lid.
2. Cook the drink on Low for 5 hours. Stir it every 2 hours.

Nutrition Info:

- Per Serving: 364 calories, 7.8g protein, 54.g carbohydrates, 13g fat, 1g fiber, 23mg cholesterol, 138mg sodium, 200mg potassium.

Cardamom Apple Jam

Servings:4

Cooking Time: 2.5 Hours

Ingredients:

- 1 cup apples, chopped
- 1 teaspoon ground cardamom
- 2 tablespoons brown sugar
- 1 teaspoon agar

Directions:

1. Mix apples with brown sugar and transfer in the Crock Pot.
2. Leave the apples until they get the juice.
3. Then add ground cardamom and agar. Mix the mixture.
4. Close the lid and cook the jam on High for 2.5 hours.
5. Then blend the mixture until smooth and cool to room temperature.

Nutrition Info:

- Per Serving: 48 calories, 0.2g protein, 12.5g carbohydrates, 0.1g fat, 1.5g fiber, 0mg cholesterol, 2mg sodium, 72mg potassium.

Melon Pudding

Servings: 3

Cooking Time: 3 Hours

Ingredients:

- 1 cup melon, chopped
- ¼ cup of coconut milk
- 2 tablespoons cornstarch
- 1 teaspoon vanilla extract

Directions:

1. Blend the melon until smooth and mix with coconut milk, cornstarch, and vanilla extract.
2. Transfer the mixture in the Crock Pot and cook the pudding on low for 3 hours.

Nutrition Info:

- Per Serving: 88 calories, 0.9g protein, 10.4g carbohydrates, 4.9g fat, 1g fiber, 0mg cholesterol, 12mg sodium, 194mg potassium.

Amaretto Pear Butter

Servings: 6

Cooking Time: 6 1/2 Hours

Ingredients:

- 4 pounds ripe pears, peeled, cored and sliced
- 1 1/2 cups white sugar
- 1/4 cup dark brown sugar
- 1/4 cup Amaretto liqueur
- 1/2 teaspoon cinnamon powder

Directions:

1. Combine all the ingredients in your Crock Pot.
2. Cover the pot and cook on low settings for 6 hours.
3. When done, pour the batter in your glass jars and seal with a lid while still hot.
4. Allow to cool before serving.

Dates And Rice Pudding

Servings: 2

Cooking Time: 3 Hours

Ingredients:

- 1 cup dates, chopped
- ½ cup white rice
- 1 cup almond milk
- 2 tablespoons brown sugar
- 1 teaspoon almond extract

Directions:

1. In your Crock Pot, mix the rice with the milk and the other ingredients, whisk, put the lid on and cook on Low for 3 hours.
2. Divide the pudding into bowls and serve.

Nutrition Info:

- calories 152, fat 5, fiber 2, carb 6, protein 3

Cardamom Apples

Servings: 2

Cooking Time: 2 Hours

Ingredients:

- 1 pound apples, cored and cut into wedges
- ½ cup almond milk
- ¼ teaspoon cardamom, ground
- 2 tablespoons brown sugar

Directions:

1. In your Crock Pot, mix the apples with the cardamom and the other ingredients, toss, put the lid on and cook on High for 2 hours.
2. Divide the mix into bowls and serve cold.

Nutrition Info:

- calories 280, fat 2, fiber 1, carbs 10, protein 6

Apple Granola Crumble

Servings: 4

Cooking Time: 6 1/4 Hours

Ingredients:

- 4 red apples, peeled, cored and sliced
- 2 tablespoons honey
- 1 1/2 cups granola
- 1/2 teaspoon cinnamon powder

Directions:

1. Mix the apples and honey in your crock pot.
2. Top with the granola and sprinkle with cinnamon.
3. Cover the pot and cook on low settings for 6 hours.
4. Serve the crumble warm.

Chocolate Pudding

Servings: 4

Cooking Time: 1 Hour

Ingredients:

- 4 ounces heavy cream
- 4 ounces dark chocolate, cut into chunks
- 1 teaspoon sugar

Directions:

1. In a bowl, mix the cream with chocolate and sugar, whisk well, pour into your Crock Pot, cover and cook on High for 1 hour.
2. Divide into bowls and serve cold.

Nutrition Info:

- calories 232, fat 12, fiber 6, carbs 9, protein 4

Blueberries Jam

Servings: 2

Cooking Time: 4 Hours

Ingredients:

- 2 cups blueberries
- ½ cup water
- ¼ pound sugar
- Zest of 1 lime

Directions:

1. In your Crock Pot, combine the berries with the water and the other ingredients, toss, put the lid on and cook on High for 4 hours.
2. Divide into small jars and serve cold.

Nutrition Info:

- calories 250, fat 3, fiber 2, carbs 6, protein 1

Tarragon Peach Confiture

Servings: 6

Cooking Time: 2.5 Hours

Ingredients:

- 1-pound peaches, pitted, halved
- ½ cup of sugar
- 1 teaspoon lemon zest, grated
- 1 teaspoon dried tarragon
- 1/3 cup water

Directions:

1. Put all ingredients in the Crock Pot and close the lid.
2. Cook the dessert on high for 5 hours.
3. Cool the cooked confiture well.

Nutrition Info:

- Per Serving: 73 calories, 0.3g protein, 19.1g carbohydrates, 0.1g fat, 0.4g fiber, 0mg cholesterol, 0mg sodium, 52mg potassium.

Lentil Pudding

Servings: 4

Cooking Time: 6 Hours

Ingredients:

- ½ cup green lentils
- 3 cups of milk
- 2 tablespoons of liquid honey
- 1 teaspoon vanilla extract
- 1 teaspoon cornflour

Directions:

1. Put all ingredients in the Crock Pot and carefully mix.
2. Close the lid and cook the pudding on Low for 6 hours.
3. Cool the pudding to the room temperature and transfer in the serving bowls.

Nutrition Info:

- Per Serving: 213 calories, 12.3g protein, 32.7g carbohydrates, 4g fat, 7.4g fiber, 15mg cholesterol, 88mg sodium, 343mg potassium.

Pear Apple Jam

Servings: 12

Cooking Time: 3 Hrs.

Ingredients:

- 8 pears, cored and cut into quarters
- 2 apples, peeled, cored and quartered
- ½ cup apple juice
- 1 tsp cinnamon, ground

Directions:

1. Toss pears, apples, apple juice, and cinnamon in the insert of Crock Pot.
2. Put the cooker's lid on and set the cooking time to 3 hours on High settings.
3. Blend this cooked pears-apples mixture to make a jam.
4. Allow it to cool them divide in the jars.
5. Serve.

Nutrition Info:

- Per Serving: Calories: 100, Total Fat: 1g, Fiber: 2g, Total Carbs: 20g, Protein: 3g

Bounty

Servings: 6

Cooking Time: 20 Minutes

Ingredients:

- 2 tablespoons condensed milk
- 1 tablespoon coconut oil
- 1 cup coconut shred
- 3 oz milk chocolate
- 2 tablespoons heavy cream

Directions:

1. Mix heavy cream with milk chocolate and put it in the Crock Pot.
2. Cook the mixture on High for 20 minutes or until it is melted.
3. Meanwhile, mix condensed milk with coconut oil and coconut shred.
4. Make the small sweets and freeze them for 15 minutes.
5. Then sprinkle every coconut sweet with melted chocolate mixture.

Nutrition Info:

- Per Serving: 240 calories, 3g protein, 22.7g carbohydrates, 15.6g fat, 1.8g fiber, 12mg cholesterol, 21mg sodium, 80mg potassium.

Ricotta Bake With Dates And Nuts

Servings: 3

Cooking Time: 2.5 Hours

Ingredients:

- 2 oz nuts, chopped
- 2 dates, chopped
- 1 cup ricotta cheese
- 2 tablespoons of liquid honey
- 1 egg, beaten

Directions:

1. Mix ricotta cheese with buts and eggs and transfer in the ramekins.
2. Put the ramekins in the Crock Pot and close the lid.
3. Cook the dessert on High for 2.5 hours.
4. Then top the ramekins with dates and liquid honey.

Nutrition Info:

- Per Serving: 305 calories, 14.7g protein, 24.8g carbohydrates, 17.7g fat, 2.2g fiber, 80mg cholesterol, 251mg sodium, 279mg potassium.

Braised Pears

Servings: 6

Cooking Time: 2.5 Hours

Ingredients:

- 6 pears
- 2 cups wine
- 1 tablespoon sugar
- 1 cinnamon stick

Directions:

1. Cut the pears into halves and put them in the Crock Pot.
2. Add all remaining ingredients and close the lid.
3. Cook the pears on High for 2.5 hours.
4. Serve the pears with hot wine mixture.

Nutrition Info:

- Per Serving: 210 calories, 1.1g protein, 38g carbohydrates, 1.1g fat, 6.5g fiber, 0mg cholesterol, 29mg sodium, 320mg potassium.

Cocoa Peanut Candies

Servings: 11

Cooking Time: 2.5 Hrs.

Ingredients:

- 6 tbsp, peanuts, roasted and crushed
- 8 oz dark chocolate, crushed
- ¼ cup of cocoa powder
- 4 tbsp chocolate chips
- 3 tbsp heavy cream

Directions:

1. Add roasted peanuts and rest of the ingredients to the insert of Crock Pot.
2. Put the cooker's lid on and set the cooking time to 5 hours on Low settings.
3. Divide this chocolate mixture into a silicone candy molds tray.
4. Place this tray in the refrigerator for 2 hours.
5. Serve.

Nutrition Info:

- Per Serving: Calories: 229, Total Fat: 15.8g, Fiber: 3g, Total Carbs: 19.02g, Protein: 5g

Banana Muffins

Servings: 2

Cooking Time: 2.5 Hours

Ingredients:

- 2 eggs, beaten
- 2 bananas, chopped
- 4 tablespoons flour
- ½ teaspoon vanilla extract
- ½ teaspoon baking powder

Directions:

1. Mash the chopped bananas and mix them with eggs.
2. Then add vanilla extract and baking powder.
3. Add flour and stir the mixture until smooth.
4. Pour the banana mixture in the muffin molds (fill ½ part of every muffin mold) and transfer in the Crock Pot.
5. Cook the muffins on High for 2.5 hours.

Nutrition Info:

- Per Serving: 229 calories, 84g protein, 39.9g carbohydrates, 4.9g fat, 3.5g fiber, 164mg cholesterol, 64mg sodium, 626mg potassium.

Caramel Sauce Poached Pears

Servings: 6

Cooking Time: 6 1/2 Hours

Ingredients:

- 6 ripe but firm pears, peeled and cored
- 1 1/2 cups caramel sauce
- 1 1/2 cups white wine
- 1 cinnamon stick
- 1 pinch salt

Directions:

1. Combine all the ingredients in your crock pot.
2. Cover the pot and cook on low settings for 6 hours.
3. Allow the pears to cool in the cooking liquid before serving.

Baked Camembert

Servings: 6

Cooking Time: 1.5 Hours

Ingredients:

- 1-pound camembert
- 1 oz walnuts, chopped
- 2 tablespoons of liquid honey

Directions:

1. Line the Crock Pot with baking paper.
2. Then put the camembert in the bottom of the Crock Pot and close the lid.
3. Cook the meal on High for 1.5 hours.
4. Then make the circle in the camembert with the help of the knife.
5. Sprinkle the cooked cheese with liquid honey and walnuts.

Nutrition Info:

- Per Serving: 277 calories, 16.1g protein, 6.6g carbohydrates, 21.1g fat, 0.3g fiber, 54mg cholesterol, 637mg sodium, 170mg potassium.

Blueberry Tapioca Pudding

Servings:4

Cooking Time: 3 Hours

Ingredients:

- 4 teaspoons blueberry jam
- 4 tablespoons tapioca
- 2 cups of milk

Directions:

1. Mix tapioca with milk and pour it in the Crock Pot.
2. Close the lid and cook the liquid on low for 3 hours.
3. Then put the blueberry jam in 4 ramekins.
4. Cool the cooked tapioca pudding until warm and pour over the jam.

Nutrition Info:

- Per Serving: 112 calories, 4.1g protein, 18.8g carbohydrates, 2.5g fat, 0.1g fiber, 10mg cholesterol, 58mg sodium, 71mg potassium.

Fluffy Vegan Cream

Servings:6

Cooking Time: 1.5 Hours

Ingredients:

- 1 cup coconut cream
- 1 avocado, pitted, peeled, chopped
- ½ cup of soy milk
- 1 tablespoon corn starch

Directions:

1. Pour soy milk in the Crock Pot.
2. Add corn starch and stir until smooth.
3. Then close the lid and cook the liquid on high for 1.5 hours.
4. Meanwhile, whip the coconut cream and blend the avocado.
5. Mix the blended avocado with thick soy milk mixture and then carefully mix it with whipped coconut cream.

Nutrition Info:

- Per Serving: 363 calories, 4.2g protein, 14.5g carbohydrates, 33.7g fat, 2.8g fiber, 0mg cholesterol, 13mg sodium, 206mg potassium.

Conclusion

In conclusion, the Crock Pot stands out as an essential kitchen appliance that offers a plethora of benefits for home cooks of all skill levels. Its versatility, ease of use, and ability to enhance the flavors of a wide variety of dishes make it a valuable addition to any kitchen. The slow cooking process allows for the development of complex flavors and tender textures, making it ideal for preparing everything from hearty soups and stews to delightful desserts. By understanding how to utilize this appliance effectively, cooks can maximize its features and seamlessly incorporate it into their meal preparation routine, leading to a more enjoyable cooking experience.

Moreover, the Crock Pot encourages culinary exploration and creativity, inviting cooks to try new recipes, experiment with different ingredients, and discover the joys of slow cooking. This appliance opens up a world of possibilities, allowing you to prepare dishes that are not only delicious but also nutritionally balanced. Sharing a meal prepared in the Crock Pot fosters a sense of connection and togetherness among family and friends, transforming ordinary dinners into special occasions filled with warmth and love. The satisfaction of coming home to a perfectly cooked meal, ready to be shared with loved ones, cannot be overstated.

As you embrace the wonders of slow cooking, you will find that the Crock Pot not only simplifies your meal preparation but also enriches your culinary journey, making it easier to enjoy wholesome, home-cooked meals without the stress of time constraints. Ultimately, the Crock Pot serves as a testament to the joys of home cooking, allowing you to savor every bite while creating lasting memories around the dining table. Whether you're a seasoned cook or just starting out, the Crock Pot is your trusty companion in the kitchen, making it possible to create delicious, nourishing meals that bring people together and celebrate the love of good food.

MEASUREMENT CONVERSIONS

BASIC KITCHEN CONVERSIONS & EQUIVALENT

DRY MEASUREMENTS CONVERSION CHART
3 TEASPOONS = 1 TABLESPOON = 1/16 CUP
6 TEASPOONS = 2 TABLESPOONS = 1/8 CUP
12 TEASPOONS = 4 TABLESPOONS = 1/4 CUP
24 TEASPOONS = 8 TABLESPOONS = 1/2 CUP
36 TEASPOONS = 12 TABLESPOONS = 3/4 CUP
48 TEASPOONS = 16 TABLESPOONS = 1 CUP

METRIC TO US COOKING CONVER SIONS

OVEN TEMPERATURE
120℃ = 250° F
160℃ = 320° F
180℃ = 350° F
205℃ = 400° F
220℃ = 425° F

OVEN TEMPERATURE
8 FLUID OUNCES = 1 CUP = 1/2 PINT = 1/4 QUART
16 FLUID OUNCES = 2 CUPS = 1 PINT = 1/2 QUART
32 FLUID OUNCES = 4 CUPS = 2 PINTS = 1 QUART= 1/4 GALLON
128 FLUID OUNCES = 16 CUPS = 8 PINTS = 4 QUARTS = 1 GALLON

BAKING IN GRAMS
1 CUP FLOUR = 140 GRAMS
1 CUP SUGAR = 150 GRAMS
1 CUP POWDERED SUGAR = 160 GRAMS
1 CUP HEAVY CREAM = 235 GRAMS

VOLUME
1 CUP FLOUR = 140 GRAMS
1 CUP SUGAR = 150 GRAMS
1 CUP POWDERED SUGAR = 160 GRAMS
1 CUP HEAVY CREAM = 235 GRAMS

WEIGHT

1 GRAM = .035 OUNCES	
100 GRAMS = 3.5 OUNCES	
500 GRAMS = 1.1 POUNDS	
1 KILOGRAM = 35 OUNCES	

BUTTER

1 CUP BUTTER = 2 STICKS = 8 OUNCES = 230 GRAMS = 8 TABLESPOONS

BUTTER

1 CUP = 8 FLUID OUNCES
1 CUP = 16 TABLESPOONS
1 CUP = 48 TEASPOONS
1 CUP = 1/2 PINT
1 CUP = 1/4 QUART
1 CUP = 1/16 GALLON
1 CUP = 240 ML

BAKING PAN CONVERSIONS

9-INCH ROUND CAKE PAN = 12 CUPS
10-INCH TUBE PAN = 16 CUPS
11-INCH BUNDT PAN = 12 CUPS
9-INCH SPRINGFORM PAN = 10 CUPS
9 X 5 INCH LOAF PAN = 8 CUPS
9-INCH SQUARE PAN = 8 CUPS

US TO METRIC COOKING CONVERSIONS

1/5 TSP = 1 ML
1 TSP = 5 ML
1 TBSP = 15 ML
1 FL OUNCE = 30 ML
1 CUP = 237 ML
1 PINT (2 CUPS) = 473 ML
1 QUART (4 CUPS) = .95 LITER
1 GALLON (16 CUPS) = 3.8 LITERS
1 OZ = 28 GRAMS
1 POUND = 454 GRAMS

US TO METRIC COOKING CONVERSIONS

1/5 TSP = 1 ML
1 TSP = 5 ML
1 TBSP = 15 ML
1 FL OUNCE = 30 ML
1 CUP = 237 ML
1 PINT (2 CUPS) = 473 ML
1 QUART (4 CUPS) = .95 LITER
1 GALLON (16 CUPS) = 3.8 LITERS
1 OZ = 28 GRAMS
1 POUND = 454 GRAMS

HEALTE RECORD TRACKER

How to Reduce Food Waste

Plan Meals: Create a weekly meal plan and shopping list.

Store Food Properly: Use airtight containers and maintain the right temperature.

FIFO Rule: Consume older items before newer ones.

Portion Control: Serve smaller portions to avoid leftovers.

Use Leftovers: Repurpose or freeze them.

Understand Expiry Dates: Many foods are safe past these dates.

Composting: Start a compost bin for food scraps.

Donate: Share surplus non-perishables with food banks.

Shop Mindfully: Buy in bulk, choose minimal packaging.

Batch Cooking: Prep and freeze meals for later.

Preserve Foods: Learn canning, pickling, and drying.

Spread Awareness: Educate and inspire others.

Recipe for:

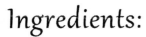

Ingredients:

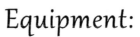

Equipment:

Description:

Instructions:

Recipe ....

From the kicthen of ....

Serves .... Prep time .... Cook time ....

☐ Difficulty   ☐ Easy   ☐ Medium   ☐ Hard

Ingredient

....

....

....

....

....

Directions ....

....

....

....

....

....

....

Recipe ....

From the kicthen of ....

Serves .... Prep time .... Cook time ....

☐ Difficulty   ☐ Easy   ☐ Medium   ☐ Hard

Ingredient   Yummy

·   ·

·   ·

·   ·

·   ·

·   ·

Directions ·

· ·

· ·

· ·

· ·

· ·

· ·

RECIPES

DATE

RECIPES		Salads	Meats	Soups
SERVES		Grains	Seafood	Snack
PREP TIME		Breads	Vegetables	Breakfast
COOK TIME		Appetizers	Desserts	Lunch
FROM THE KITCHEN OF		Main Dishes	Beverages	Dinners

INGREDIENTS

DIRECTIONS

NOTES

SERVING ☆☆☆☆☆

DIFFICULTY ☆☆☆☆☆

OVERALL ☆☆☆☆☆

APPENDIX : RECIPES INDEX

A

Asparagus Egg Casserole 15

Apricot Butter 18

Apricot Glazed Gammon 22

Asparagus Casserole 22

Apple Cups 26

Asian Sesame Chicken 43

Apples Sauté 57

Artichoke Dip 57

Asian Broccoli Sauté 62

Almond Buns 68

Almond Bowls 70

Apple Dip 70

Almond Spread 71

Apple Sausage Snack 71

Apple Jelly Sausage Snack 73

Avocado Jelly 76

Amaretto Pear Butter 77

Apple Granola Crumble 78

B

Breakfast Meat Rolls 14

Broccoli Omelet 16

Baby Carrots In Syrup 17

Bacon Eggs 17

Blue Cheese Chicken 21

Beans-rice Mix 23

Butter Buckwheat 24

Beans And Peas Bowl 27

Basil Beef 32

Beef Pot Roast 36

Buffalo Chicken Tenders 42

Bacon Chicken Wings 45

Butter Smelt 48

Butter Salmon 49

Butter Tilapia 49

Butter Crab 51

Braised Sesame Spinach 58

Buffalo Cremini Mushrooms 60

Baked Onions 63

Bean Dip 66

Beans Spread 69

Beer And Cheese Dip 71

Bourbon Sausage Bites 73

Blueberries Jam 78

Bounty 79

Braised Pears 80

Baked Camembert 81

Banana Muffins 81

Blueberry Tapioca Pudding 82

C

Carrot Pudding 13

Creamy Yogurt 13

Chia Oatmeal 17

Chicken Omelet 18

Caramel Pecan Sticky Buns 19

Chicken Meatballs 19

Cumin Rice 21

Coffee Beef Roast 22

Cherry Rice 23

Cauliflower Mashed Potatoes 25

Cider Braised Chicken 25

Crock Pot Steamed Rice 25

Creamy Polenta 26

Chicken Drumsticks And Buffalo Sauce 27

Creamed Sweet Corn 28

Chili Beef Sausages 31

Crockpot Moroccan Beef 33

Cajun Beef 36

Cheesy Pork Casserole 36

Chicken Wings In Vodka Sauce 39

Chicken Stuffed With Plums 40

Chicken Masala 41

Chicken With Basil And Tomatoes 41

Chicken And Green Onion Sauce 43

Chicken Provolone 45

Crab Legs 48

Chili Salmon 52

Crockpot Greek Snapper 52

Cinnamon Catfish 53

Creamy Pangasius 53

Creamy Puree 60

Creamy White Mushrooms 61

Curry Couscous 62

Cauliflower Curry 63

Cauliflower Rice 64

Caramel Milk Dip 66

Cinnamon Pecans Snack 66

Crispy Sweet Potatoes With Paprika 69

Cheese Onion Dip 72

Cinnamon Plum Jam 75

Clove Pastry Wheels 75

Cardamom Apple Jam 76

Cardamom Apples 77

Chocolate Pudding 78

Cocoa Peanut Candies 80

Caramel Sauce Poached Pears 81

D

Dates And Rice Pudding 77

E

Eggs With Brussel Sprouts 14

Easy Chicken Continental 46

Eggplant Parmesan Casserole 59

Egg Cauliflower 61

F

French Onion Sandwich Filling 23

Flank Steak With Arugula 33

Fluffy Vegan Cream 82

G

Green Enchilada Pork Roast 24

Garlic Duck 39

Garlic Pulled Chicken 45

Ginger Cod 49

Garlic Perch 54

Garlic Tuna 55

Garlic Gnocchi 57

Garlic Asparagus 61

Green Peas Puree 63

H

Ham Pockets 12

Honey Beef Sausages 35

Halved Chicken 44

Horseradish Chicken Wings 44

K

Kale Cups 13

Kebab Cubes 30

L

Leek Bake 12

Leek Eggs 15

Lemon Garlic Dump Chicken 39

Lemony Chicken 40

Lemony Shrimps In Hoisin Sauce 48

Lemony Artichokes 68

Lentil Pudding 79

M

Milk Pudding 18

Mango Chutney Pork Chops 22

Milky Semolina 25

Mexican Bubble Pizza 31

Mole Pork Chops 37

Mediterranean Stuffed Chicken 44

Mustard Cod 54

Mushroom Steaks 58

Mashed Turnips 59

Marshmallow Hot Drink 76

Melon Pudding 77

O

Olive Eggs 19

One Pot Pork Chops 30

Onion Dip(3) 67

Orange Bowls 75

P

Peach Puree 14

Pesto Pork Chops 35

Pork Tenderloin And Apples 35

Pesto Salmon 50

Poached Catfish 54

Paprika Okra 58

Paprika Baby Carrot 62

Pear Apple Jam 79

R

Red Salsa Chicken 27

Rosemary Pork 32

Roast And Pepperoncinis 34

Rosemary Rotisserie Chicken 41

Roasted Parmesan Green Beans 67

Ricotta Bake With Dates And Nuts 80

S

Seafood Eggs 12

Smoked Salmon Omelet 15

Squash Bowls 16

Sweet Quinoa 16

Sweet Farro 21

Sweet Popcorn 24

Salted Caramel Rice Pudding 26

Spiced Beef 31

Salsa Meat 32

Stuffed Jalapenos 33

Skirt Steak With Red Pepper Sauce 34

Sweet Beef 34

Shredded Pork 37

Soy Beef Steak 37

Salsa Chicken Wings 40

Stuffed Chicken Fillets 42

Sun-dried Tomato Chicken 42

Shrimps Boil 50

Soy Sauce Catfish 50

Spicy Curried Shrimps 51

Salmon Stew 52

Scallops With Sour Cream And Dill 55

Spicy Basil Shrimp 55

Sauteed Spinach 60

Sautéed Greens 64

Spinach With Halloumi Cheese Casserole 64

Spaghetti Squash 68

Salsa Beans Dip 69

Salmon Bites 70

Spicy Dip 70

Slow-cooked Lemon Peel 71

Spinach And Walnuts Dip 72

Spinach Dip(2) 72

T

Tomato Soy Glazed Chicken 28

Tender Pork Chops 30

Tender Duck Fillets 46

Turkey With Plums 46

Thyme And Sesame Halibut 51

Taco Mahi Mahi 53

Tarragon Peach Confiture 78

V

Vegetarian Red Coconut Curry 59

W

Wine Chicken 43

White Bean Spread 67

Made in the USA
Columbia, SC
26 December 2024

50667383R00054